EARLY VICTORIAN ALFRISTON

W H JOHNSON

DOWNSWAY BOOKS

First published in 1993 by
DOWNSWAY BOOKS
9 White Court, Kings Ride,
Alfriston, East Sussex, BN26 5XP

Reprinted 1994

Typeset by MCM, Alfriston
Printed in Century 702 pt PS
Printed and bound by
CBS Multicopies Ltd, Hailsham

British Library Cataloguing in Publication Data

A catalogue record for this book is available
from the British Library

ISBN 0 9518564 3 X

The maps overleaf are from the 1874 Ordnance Survey

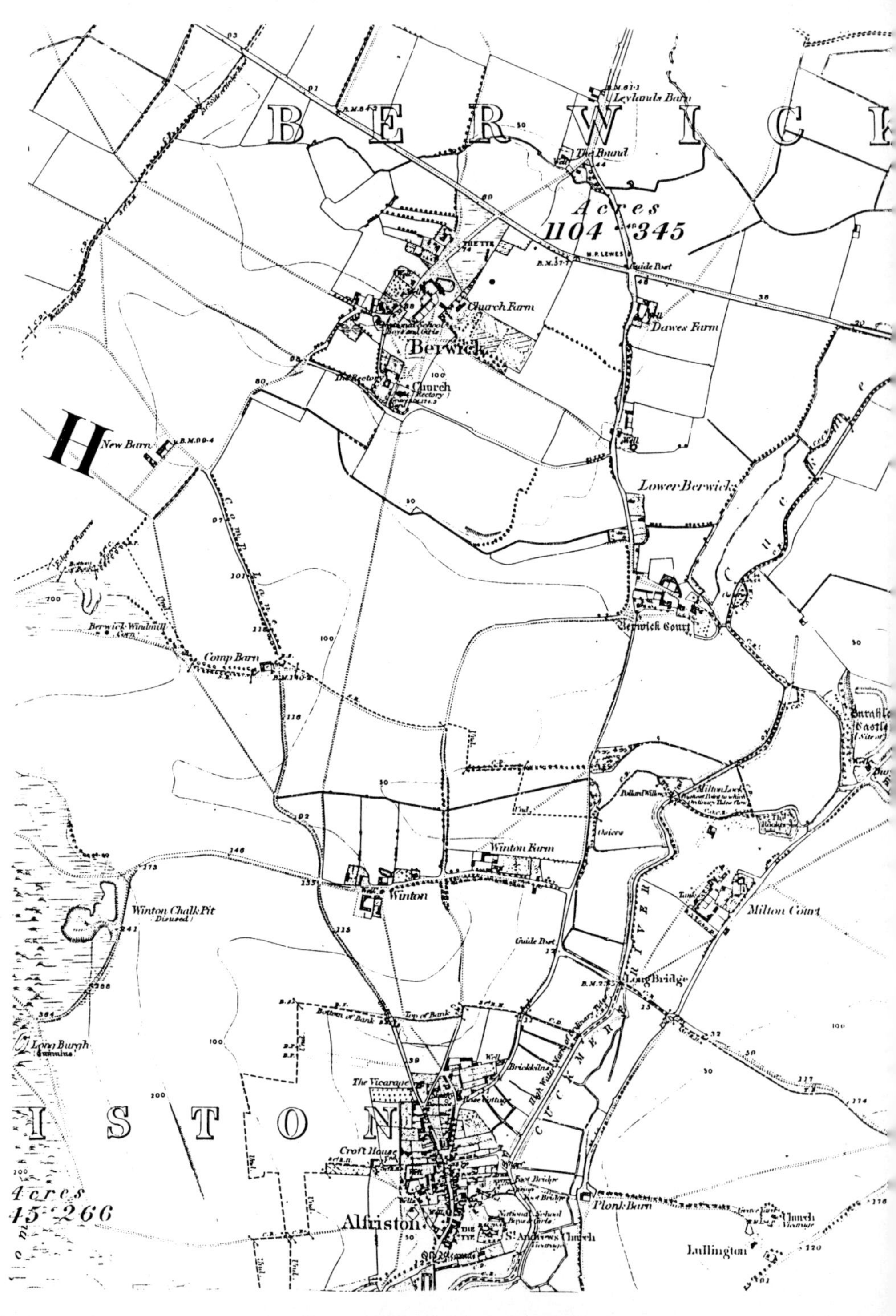
BERWICK
Acres
1104·345
Leylands Barn
The Pound
Guide Post
Church Farm
Dawes Farm
Berwick
The Rectory
Church
New Barn
H
Lower Berwick
Berwick Court
Berwick Windmill
Comp Barn
Winton Farm
Winton
Winton Chalk Pit
(Disused)
Milton Lock
Milton Court
The Rookery
Osiers
Guide Post
Long Bridge
Long Burgh
Tumulus
Top of Bank
Bottom of Bank
The Vicarage
Brickkilns
ISTON
Croft House
Acres
45·266
Alfriston
National School
Boys & Girls
St. Andrews Church
Foot Bridge
Plonk Barn
Lullington
Church
CUCKMERE RIVER

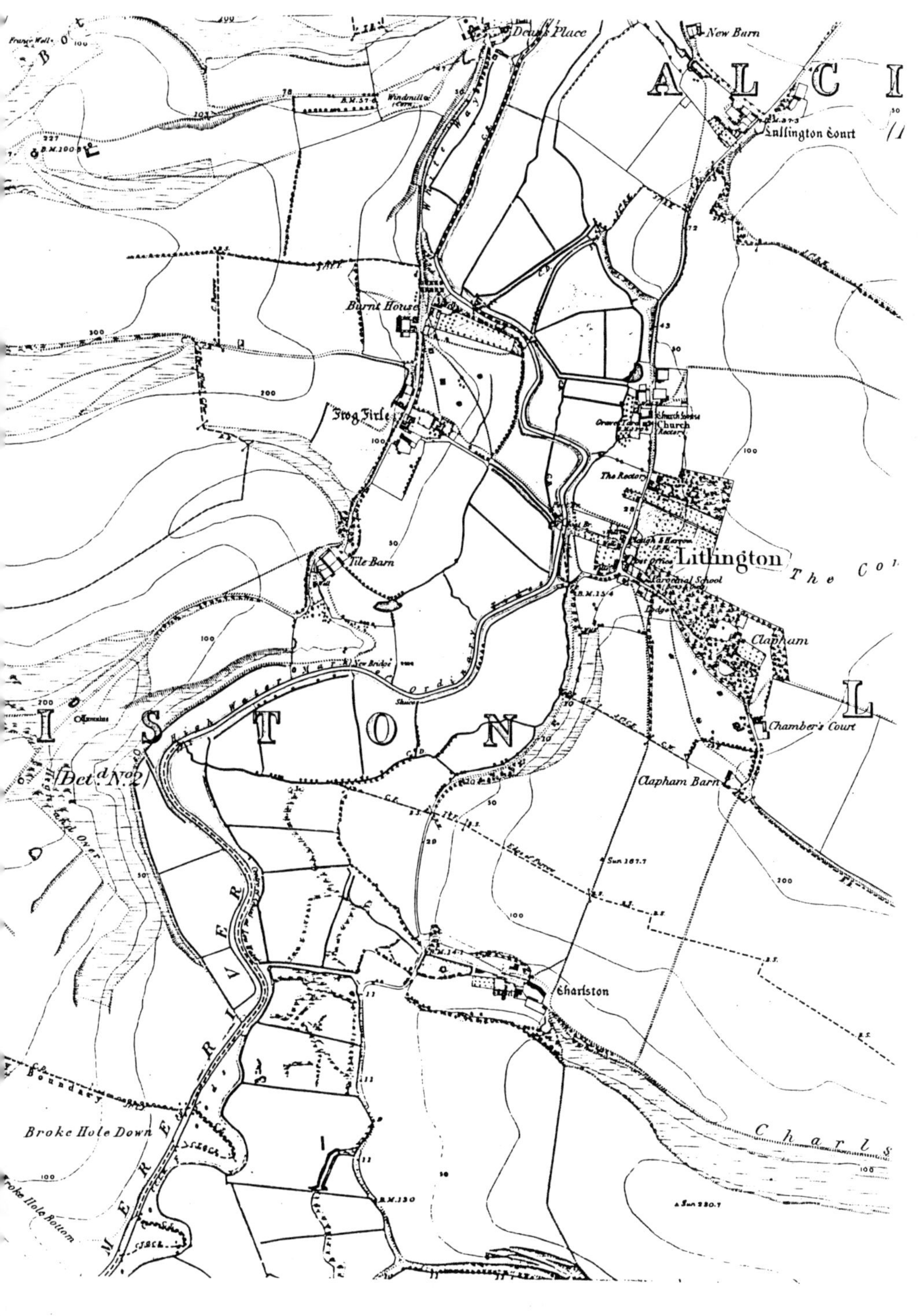

Deans Place
New Barn
ALCI
Windmill (Corn)
Lullington Court
Burnt House
Frog Firle
Church
The Rectory
Litlington
Post Office
Parochial School
Tile Barn
Plough & Harrow
Clapham
Chamber's Court
Clapham Barn
New Bridge
Sluice
STON
(Detd No. 2)
The Co
L
RIVER
MERE
Charlston
Broke Hole Down
Broke Hole Bottom
Boundary
Charls

The map on the page opposite is based on the 1843 Tithe Map of which there are only three copies. These large hand-drawn maps can be consulted in the Records Offices in Lewes, Chichester and London.

In this version, several sites mentioned in the text are identified.

1. Woolgar's Forge (Heritage Centre)
2. Rose Cottage
3. Fellmongery
4. Wharf
5. Saddlery (Saddlers Tea Rooms)
6. The Star
7. Griffin's Forge (High Street/Star Lane)
8. The George
9. Independent Chapel
10. Tannery (Tanneries and Gun Room)
11. Church and National School
12. Malthouse (Goosies)
13. Deans Place Farm

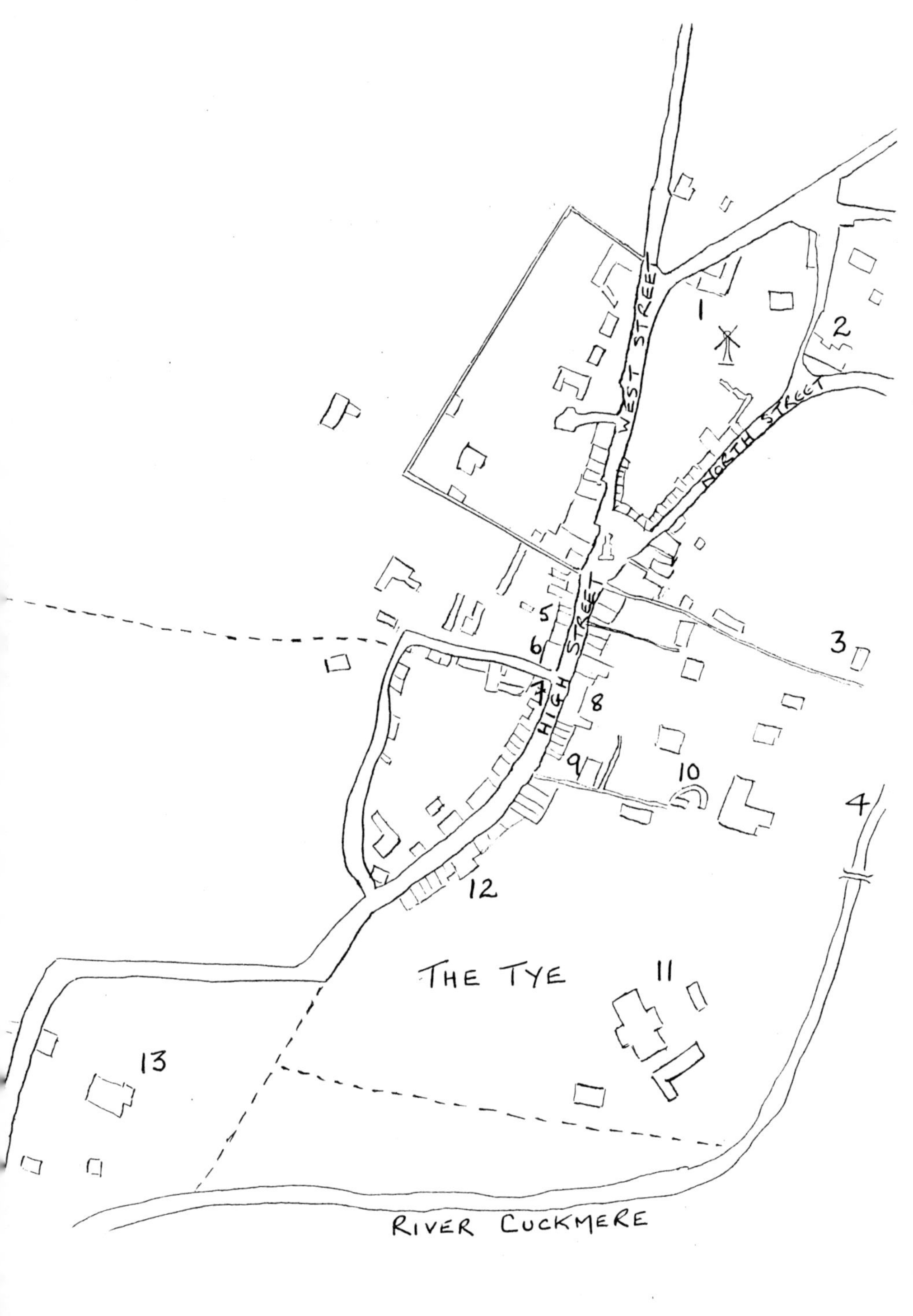
WEST STREET
NORTH STREET
HIGH STREET
1
2
3
4
5
6
7
8
9
10
11
12
13
THE TYE
RIVER CUCKMERE

ILLUSTRATIONS

The illustrations in this book are taken from:

Microcosm, W H Pyne, 1808

A General View of the Agriculture of Sussex, Rev Arthur Young, 1813

Sketches of Rural Affairs, SPCK, 1845

Illustrations of Useful Arts, Manufactures and Trades, Charles Tomlinson, 1854

I am grateful to the Museum of English Rural Life, University of Reading for their help in the selection of illustrations and equally grateful to East Sussex Record Office for enabling me to use Mark Antony Lower's 1850 drawing of The Star Inn.

INTRODUCTION

It is my purpose in writing this account of Early Victorian Alfriston to offer glimpses of some aspects of life and work in the years before the Great Exhibition; before the completion of the Lewes to Eastbourne railway; before the abolition of the Corn Laws. These are crude and wavering boundary markers indicating that such a task as mine cannot have too precise a limit. I choose these events, however, partly for their symbolic value, partly for their real-life significance.

The 1851 Exhibition signalled to the world the status of the first modern industrial nation: it signalled to Alfriston's poor the crippling realisation that rural industry and their part in it was no longer to be of such permanent and profound economic importance. In its turn, the railway, completed in 1849, was part of that first powerful instrument that narrowed down the world, that destroyed distance: some in Alfriston it would beckon to new horizons though on the village labourer it would have little obvious impact. Until many years later, when he might be called on two occasions to serve his King and Country, he would never travel far beyond his birthplace. The abolition of the Corn Laws in 1846 fractured Toryism and gave cheaper bread to the industrial towns: yet the grim warnings of awful consequences were not realised and farming's Golden Age proceeded save that Alfriston's village poor seem to have derived little benefit from it. The distress and deprivation which had begun to manifest themselves at the end of the eighteenth century would stay with them for a hundred years and more. Nineteenth century England, in parts no less than a sullen rural slum, served to demonstrate that not everyone prospered in times of progress. Exhibitions, railways, votes in Parliament might indirectly touch upon everyday life but they would have no obvious improving effect upon the lives of ordinary country families.

And the earlier limits? These are even more distant, just discernible in the late eighteenth century with the changes in local agriculture; in the wars against Bonaparte with their profits for Alfriston's astute tradesmen and farmers; in the post-war years, into the 1830s, in the waste land of deflation, deterioration and distress.

These then are the external limits. I certainly admit to straying into the years long before 1837 and I rely on some sources later than what may justly be called Early Victorian. But to describe the period seems to me to be impossible unless I allow myself such licence.

Now for a tighter focus on our parish although I cannot promise a definitive picture, neither a detailed portrait nor even a sharp edged silhouette. Glimpses, I have said, no more than that, for the sources are not generous. There are no diaries, letters, account books. Still, there are the 1841 Census and the 1843 Tithe Map, both of which are invaluable for what they tell us though frustrating in their silences. It is from these two documents that I have made my beginning: these are the major sources from which I have tried to build up this account of Early Victorian Alfriston. What emerges is a kind of micro-history, for I have really aimed to locate it, despite my roving across the years, in a narrow period of time and within the bounds of one small parish. I am compelled to speculate and hope that I have not lost everything in a haze of generalisation. There are gaps, in part the fault of people a hundred and fifty years ago who left no records because they had no warning of my intention to write about them. Other gaps, I fear, are a consequence of my own ignorance which I hope will not mar the reader's enjoyment.

In 'Our Sussex Parish' Thomas Geering, born in the village, writes: "The history of the parish must, like that of a nation, be the history of the people". I have kept that in mind in this piece of reconstruction. I hope that by putting the spotlight for a few brief moments on some of history's bit-part players, I can represent them and their lives with some degree of accuracy and respect.

I have very frequently inserted modern names of houses in brackets in order to help readers who wish to locate precisely where they were. Thus, this is a kind of guide book too. It may be helpful to our many visitors for the village is high on the list of tourist venues in East Sussex. Our present contrasts strangely with our past.

I am grateful to many local people, some of whom have offered me information and advice of real importance. Without exception, all of those with whom I have discussed this project have shown interest in it and have thereby encouraged me more than they can know. I am especially grateful to Joan Wayne and Julian Tayler for their most helpful observations on the draft text. My thanks, too, to Mary Morton, for yet again interpreting my uncertain handwriting and producing the manuscript in good order.

W.H. Johnson
Alfriston

July 1993

The road from Seaford winds and switchbacks its way across and down the northern slope of Hindover, past Tile Barn and Frog Firle and Burnt House. All along our route, on the left, has been the swelling rise of the downs, on the right the water meadows and the snaking Cuckmere River. Then, when we reach what was once Deans Place Farm, the church spire breaks the skyline and suddenly we are into the High Street. Most of the buildings on each side of us were there in the eighteenth century, many long before. On our right is 'The George', one of the oldest buildings in the village, and like 'The Star' which faces it, its antiquity has been emphasised by modern artifice. Ahead is Waterloo Square and the market cross, another ancient landmark, and here the road divides.

To our left is West Street. A hundred and fifty years ago, fields and gardens began where the horseshoe of the Square ended. There were cottages on the opposite side, still there today, and beyond them what Alfriston-born Thomas Geering described as the "better looking houses on the old Berwick Road", where Dr Sanger and Kidd the saddler lived. Ahead on the right is the one-time Vicarage and the cluster of houses around Sloe Lane.

Behind the High Street is the Tye, today the village green, but at the time of Victoria's accession, pastureland belonging to Deans Place Farm. Here is the church dedicated to St Andrew and the one time Schoolroom (War Memorial Hall).

The fork to the right of Waterloo Square leads down North Street. On the left hand side are more cottages; then the house (Badgers) where the Haryotts for so many years baked bread and made shoes and after that what was, until 1834, the Parish Poor House (Workhouse Cottage). There are some more substantial old houses before us: Brook Furlong, Rose Cottage, Little Dene and The Dene and then a scattering of cottages takes us to where the road leads off to Longbridge and on to the houses up Winton Street.

Thus, our small world, from Hindover to Winton Street, its limits north and south, from one end to the other perhaps four miles. The river marks our eastern edge whilst the western boundary straggles over open downland to enclose about 2,700 acres; nor have these boundaries shifted much in several hundred years.

Let Florence Pagden, born in 1863, describe the parish boundaries. Let us hear the old names as she knew them.

> "Starting then from the Cross Stone, to the South, passing Dean's Place, we come to the White Way, supposed to be haunted by a white dog. Then the gentle rise is called Duke's Green Hill. Past Frog Firle, we come to a steep descent called West Hill leading to Tile Barn and so up again by Shepherd's Road and on to Seaford.
>
> "Northward from the Market Cross, we go down West Street, formerly called Catt Street - no doubt belonging to that family - past the Vicarage and the Forge, we come to a narrow lane, once the High Road, called Sloe Field Hedge and on to Snake and Adder Lane. We cross Winton Street and the road leads to the present High Road to Berwick."

How inaccessible the village was, a minor port - even that description sounds too grand - on a scarce known river, or reached by narrow roads, often little more than muddy tracks. Certainly, the rutted roadway to the outer world had to be maintained, even if at minimum cost. It was part of the old Glynde Bridge route which, skirting the foot of the downs via West Firle, Alciston, Berwick and Winton Street, finally terminated at Longbridge. From there, though unsurfaced, it passed through Milton Street and up to the fast, easily graded Lewes to Eastbourne turnpike. Another route, difficult enough, went across Windover and down into Jevington, and thence to Eastbourne.

The old roads were worked on intermittently by groups of labourers, employed sometimes by farmers, at other times paid by the parish. These workmen spread flints - small enough to put in the mouth, they were instructed - on the surface as smoothly as possible. It was left to the general movement of traffic, to the passage of countless iron-rimmed cart wheels, to smooth them down. In summer, of course, the roads threw up great clouds of dust; in winter, they were churned into mud tracks. Even the village streets had to be negotiated with care although Lower's drawing of 'The Star' in 1850 hints at firmly bedded stones and a gutter. When Thomas Geering's mother was married at St Andrew's Church at the beginning of the century she wore her best dress for the occasion. At the same time, on her feet she wore pattens, those wooden soled slip-ons with a deep iron rim which raised the wearer another two or three inches above the surface mud.

The roads were fit for slow-moving traffic, for coaches and ox-drawn farm carts, for market-bound cattle, for travellers on horseback. These were essential routes for Thomas Carter, the carrier from Sloe Lane. It was his valuable service which linked the village with Lewes and Hailsham. He made deliveries of skins and flour; he was called upon for house removals; his regular service took passengers to outlying markets although he would rarely travel out more than fifteen miles. John Baker, the rag-and-bone man, was often about on these roads too as was the sweep, young David Hayter. Once they reached the Lewes to Eastbourne turnpike, their journey was easier but up to there, it was hard going whatever the season.

On the Cuckmere there was little enough traffic though Joseph Lower's barge, a ten-tonner, with a rectangular sail, was a regular user. Usually, he came up on the tide, sometimes assisted by the breeze; most often, he was obliged to use his pole to achieve any speed or to get himself off the river banks. He tied up at the wharf just below River Lane and unloaded seaweed for the fields, coal, oil-cake for fattening oxen. At times he went as far as Longbridge with a load of sea-beach for the road men to lay as a base or as a filling for pot holes.

It has been suggested that there was another wharf near the Old Clergy House. This is unlikely to have been the case because of the inconvenience of unloading and the lack of good enough access for carts and wagons to carry away deliveries. It is possible, however, that Lower tied up there regularly for he rented part of the nearby Parsonage (Old Clergy House) for many years.

At one time, during the war against Bonaparte, at least two barges had worked the river. In 1841, a second man is described as a bargeman and ten years later there were two bargemen in addition to Lower. Whether this signifies two or more barges, however, cannot be said with any certainty.

Neither by road nor river was this small community easily reached. It was a backwater, yet with all the characteristics of so many rural communities throughout the land. Remote, quaintly named, small enough, yet with its variety of trades and its strong agricultural base, the parish was able to sustain itself. Until the beginning of the nineteenth century, that is. Then, and certainly by the 1830s, and despite all appearances to the contrary, it was a village in decline and from that time, its nature would change for all time.

THE STAR INN ALFRISTON, 1850.

SOME HOUSES, SOME PEOPLE

There were no more than 129 houses in the Early Victorian parish as opposed to about 360 today. For the most part, as dwellings, they were significantly smaller. The population totals, however, are remarkably similar. In 1841, 668 people were recorded as living here: today, there are about 700. The age spread, however, in those earlier days, was more regular than now. There were several 80 year olds and rather more 70 year olds; there were yet more 60 year olds and so on down the pyramid. It was overall a generally younger population and certainly there was a greater number of children than now, 120 boys and girls aged between 5 and 11 years as opposed to 80 or so today.

Inevitably, the houses were crowded. For example, a house in Weavers Lane (Sevencrofts) is roomy enough today for a family, now that it has had considerable alterations and additions. In 1841, it was a humble two-up, two-down. A family called Geering lived there. There was Maria, the mother of 15 year old Augusta, James (8), Ellen (5) and Elizabeth (2). Then there were two males, John and Charles, both men in their thirties and apparently brothers. One of them - it is unclear which - was Maria's husband. It would be possible to arrange the sleeping accommodation so that sensibilities would not be offended but at best it would be inconvenient. If the same occupants were there in, say, another half-dozen years, there might be difficulties. And, anyway, Maria, a dressmaker, needed space, having to do her cutting out and sewing and ironing in one of these rooms.

Examples are legion concerning large families at this time, brothers and sisters sleeping in the same room, cramped, lacking privacy. In one of the small cottages at Burnt House Farm, Charles Marchant lived with his wife and seven children. In the village, in Chapel Cottages, the carpenter George Ellis and his wife were bringing up nine children, the oldest of them 13 years old, the youngest 3 months. As for Dene Cottages, now two pleasant old-style houses abutting the main road, a hundred and fifty years ago, before walls were knocked down and interiors re-arranged, there were certainly four, perhaps five dwellings, here.

Right through the village, in the High Street, in West Street and North Street too, tiny cottages huddled together, dark and uncomfortable, their walls and brick floors exuding damp. At night they lit their world with candles and 'fried straws' which when extinguished produced a scarcely breathable, pungent smell.

There are no exact descriptions of the interiors of the cottages in which Alfriston's labourers lived. Elsewhere, however, labourers' homes are described as being draughty, damp, lacking drainage and adequate sanitary arrangements. There is no reason to believe Alfriston cottages to be superior to this. Here, there was no paternalistic squire to keep his workers' homes in trim. Instead, the houses were in the main owned by tradesmen who, not necessarily unkind men, regarded their properties as commercial investments and were not disposed to lay out good money on cottages which yielded little more than about £3 per year.

There is much evidence of the cramped dimensions of rural cottages. Often there was a brick paved downstairs room of, say, 20 feet by 15 feet. Sometimes this was partitioned to allow some further private sleeping place. The house might be furnished with an oak table, a mahogany cupboard, some chairs. Some attempt to prettify it with rag rugs, brass candlesticks and crockery was often evident. Upstairs, there would be not more than two bedrooms, one perhaps for adults and baby, the other for the remainder of the family, boys and girls mixed in together. In 1803, only thirty-three dwellings in Alfriston Parish had ovens. By 1840, matters had not changed.

Against the outside wall were often piles of faggots, not infrequently given in lieu of wages. A garden for vegetables might be available although this did not always satisfy a family's total needs. At times, there was a hog pen, the animal fed slops from the dishes of several joint-owning families.

There were frequent complaints, accusations, that "the diseases of the poor are to be attributed to poor living and want of cleanliness chiefly". But go back all those years. Go out into the back gardens of the High Street or Waterloo Square. Go out to the pump and fill the heavy metal bucket. Go out and lug it into the kitchen and transfer it to the biggest iron pot you have. Then go out for the next bucketful and the next. Heat them over the fire whose fuel you have had to pay for. Heat up enough if you can afford it, for your family of half a dozen and more. Do that on a regular basis when the menfolk come back from the fields. The men who wrote about your want of cleanliness had servants for that tiring, time-consuming task. Your small boy, your young daughter, carried the water from the pump for these men and their clean families. It is easy to be clean at the turn of a tap or if the working of a pump and the carrying of buckets and the heating of water is done by others.

It is difficult for us to conjure up visions of the past without the intrusion of images from the present. We are persuaded through our literature and our film and TV screens, of a kindly and cosy time, of smiling and healthy old folk and bright-eyed chubby children, a world invented by 'Hovis' or 'Disney', suffused by the rays of late afternoon sunshine, by the gentle, friendly glow of lamps. The past seems to have a rich patina. But many of these people lived closer to Chaucer and Piers Plowman than to the England of the late twentieth century. Twenty years later than the period I am dealing with, in 1867, the cottages of rural Sussex were declared in a report to the Poor Law Commissioners to be "deficient in almost every requisite that should constitute a home for a Christian family in a civilised country". Later still, in the early years of the present century, Arthur Beckett, the newspaper proprietor, pronounced his views on Alfriston. "Some of the villagers," he wrote, "live like poor Irish peasants among their animals.". If there was a Golden Age, it was unlikely to be within the experience of anyone who lived in a labourer's cottage in Alfriston in the nineteenth century.

On the other hand there were some attractive houses, nothing of course on the grand scale, but fine enough for professional men, for retired tenant farmers and for the employers of skilled craftsmen. In West Street, then called Catt Street, three substantial residences housed Dr Sanger (Tuckvar), the retired saddler William Kidd (Alfriston House) and Mrs Sarah Scrase a farmer's widow (The Chaise House).

At the north end of the village, three good-looking south-facing houses appear to have been built more or less in the same period of the eighteenth century. Mrs Sarah Brook's house (Rose Cottage) had the common brewery attached to it until 1839. The slightly smaller house of Dr Cooley (Brook Furlong) stands between it and Henry Woolgar's house and forge (The Heritage Centre).

At the other end of the village, in the High Street, lived a retired farmer and his wife, Mr and Mrs King, in a small well-proportioned house (Southdown House) and higher up the street, on the same side, Mrs Mary Newman, whose late husband had part-owned the tannery, lived in a house now known as 'The Old Apiary'.

In the Square, the saddler William Marchant's home (The Manor House) stood opposite his workshop (Saddler's Cafe). The present butcher's shop, a house with an impressive frontage, was the home of William Wright, a schoolmaster who appears to have boarded and taught pupils there. Its garden included a building in River Lane, now named 'The Coach House' which at the time was probably used to store his gig and perhaps stable his horse.

Charles Brooker, former Deacon of the Chapel, schismatic, unsuccessful parliamentary candidate, opponent of the Union Workhouse, Chartist, owner of the tannery and fellmongery, lived in what today is called Bank House Farm. Like many of the wealthier members of the community, he owned several houses and some acres of downland on which he pastured sheep.

Opposite, Market Cross House (Smugglers Inn), where Brooker's former enemy Stanton Collins had lived, was now occupied by William Banks. At various times, depending upon the document consulted, he is a brewer, a mealman or a butcher. It is not unlikely that he was all three at the same time. In the back quarters of this house, the largest in the village, was a slaughterhouse and malthouse although there is today no visible evidence that any of the buildings served these purposes. In Banks' time they were new, the deeds indicating that Collins, also a butcher, had put them up in 1826. As a mealman, Banks bought meal from the village's three millers. One of them, Daniel Sudbury, lived next door to him (Post Office).

These were homes of some substance, well furnished, stuffed with customary Victorian excess. Their dark and sombre atmosphere can be imagined. An indication of their interiors may be gleaned from the following account of the sale of effects which comes from the columns of the 'Sussex Agricultural Express'.

"ALFRISTON, SUSSEX - Genuine Household Furniture, China, Glass, Books, Linen, Oil Prints &c., Gigs, a useful Gig Horse and Harnesses; Kitchen and Culinary effects &c., &c.

TO BE SOLD BY AUCTION BY
WENHAM & SON
On Thursday and Friday, the 6th and 7th days of April 1843
on the premises.

THE NEAT HOUSEHOLD FURNITURE and other effects, by the direction of the executors of Charles Brooker, Esq., deceased, consisting of prime goose and other feather beds, hair and other mattresses, mahogany four-post, tent, and other bedsteads, with suitable furniture; stands, handsome chimney glasses in gilt frames, dressing ditto, parlour, bedroom and stair carpets; a fine toned pianoforte, by Tomkinson; mahogany dining, Pembroke, and tea tables; mahogany horse hair sofas, ditto ditto chairs, handsome book case, very handsome eight-day clock in mahogany case, two timepieces in mahogany frames, a pair of globes, oil prints of Williams and Harris the Missionaries, by Baxter; curious stuffed birds, handsome and rich old china, glass trays &c., copper coal scuttle, furnace fenders, fire irons, and the usual Kitchen and culinary requisites.

Also about 500 volumes of books chiefly on religious subjects, among which will be found the following viz. - Old Mixen's History of England, 2 vols, folio; Rapin's ditto, 2 vols, ditto; Speed's ditto, 2 vols, ditto; Universal Dictionaries of Art and Sciences, with plates and maps, 2 vols, ditto; Fox's Book of Martyrs, with plates, ditto; History of London, ditto; Cruden's Concordance, quarto; Burkett's ditto, 2 vols, ditto; Scott's Commentary, 5 vols, ditto; Sutcliff's ditto, 2 vols, ditto; Encyclopaedia Britannica, 2nd edition, with 370 plates and maps, 23 vols, ditto; the Reformation, 8 vols, ditto; Whitfield's Works; Hervey's Theron and Aspasia, &c., &c. - The sale will begin each day at 12 o'clock and the whole will be sold without reserve.

Printed catalogues may be had three days previous to the Sale, at the Bridge Inn, Newhaven; Star Inn, Lewes; Lamb Inn, Eastbourne; of Mr. J. Foster, Stationer, Uckfield; Mr. G. Woodhams, Alfriston; on the premises; and at the Auctioneers, Hailsham"

Perhaps the above notice gives a more lively appreciation of the possessions and possibly the minds of men of Brooker's station, the tenant farmers, the professional men, and the skilled tradesmen.

When a couple of years earlier the village plumber/glazier died, his effects had included:

> "... 3 good feather beds, bolsters and pillows, four post and other bedsteads and furniture, blankets, quilts, 2 pair of very good mahogany chests of drawers, linen chests and boxes, chamber tables and chairs, swing glasses, good 30-hour clock and case, double and single corner and square cupboards, good oak and other dining, tea, baking and other tables; kitchen and arm chairs, writing desk, bureau, work stand, trays, china, plates and dishes, mugs, a good barometer, 24 gallon copper furnace and fillings, boilers, pottage pots, saucepans, tin articles, knives and forks, 2 good brine tubs, barrels, water pails, warming and frying pans, block and Italian irons, coal grates, fire irons, brown earthenware, and numerous other useful and culinary articles.
>
> Also about 50 bushels of good eating potatoes, in small lots, 2 good water casks, 2 garden frames and lights, 2 hard glasses, loading cart, some books including a large Family Bible, Fox's Book of Martyrs, Cooke's Geography &c &c."

Such a substantial range of possessions was undoubtedly common among the hard-working group of tradesmen and superior artisans within the parish. These were people well able to employ servants to keep their houses in good order. They had overcome the difficulties of daily living experienced by the labouring poor in their damp, dark, overcrowded cottages.

THE SERVANTS

Something in the order of twenty of the families in the parish, those living on farms or in larger village houses, had live-in servants. If a girl, or a boy for that matter, could find a situation in a private home or in a farmhouse, away from the raw life of winter fields, away from irregular employment, that was often good enough for the parents. And manners might be learnt, etiquette, the quaint lore of knives and which one to use, of forks and spoons and which way to hold them. Parents might hope that such a step-up in life might lead to better things, a kind of daintiness might rub-off. Already there was the view that clean-handed work for boys, no matter how mundane the tasks, was infinitely superior to laying a hedge or repairing a plough or leading animals.

Young boys worked often in the "back'us", cleaning cutlery or scrubbing pots and pans and, if they were strong enough to manage it, carrying water from the pump down the yard to the scullery. Here was the boy's domain although he might also be called upon to run errands, polish harness, scrub benches. Edward Ellman, vicar of Berwick, required his young male servant to tend the garden and to take the vegetables and sell them at Lewes market. Very often boys like these ended up in other jobs, but often on farms, sometimes looking back with affection upon their days in the master's house. Others of them graduated into a species of rustic valet, capable of brushing a jacket, ironing trousers, driving a trap and doubling up as a majordomo. There were boy servants at Deans Place Farm and Winton Farm and Dr Sanger, in addition to two female servants, also employed a boy.

Some of the female servants then working in Alfriston houses, such as Mary Bonney and Harriet Apps seem alien to the village. There is no one else of their names. It was sometimes the case that girls came from other areas to work but this was more common where there were great estates and grand residences. But there were no such places in this parish. There was though a powerful instinct among Poor Law officials to place workhouse girls with private families, thus taking them off the parish books. Were both

Bonney and Apps recruited in this way?

What is understandable is that local girls from the least respectable homes were less likely to find such employment inside village houses. It was enough recommendation in many households for a girl to be from a regular church- or chapel-going family. For instance, Mrs Mary Newman and Charles Brooker, those pillars of the chapel, both employed daughters of chapel members and others also among the two congregations recruited similarly. The girls who went into service - although the census indicates only those girls who slept in the house and makes no reference to 'dailies' - seem to have had parents who provided for them as best they could, who brought them up ready to serve others whom they recognised to be their betters. There was no shame in service.

The servant girls - starting work, some of them at the age of eight at 6d a week, "tuck aprons and pattens provided" - had heavy restrictions placed upon them by their employers. They were often not allowed out in the evenings. Sometimes they had no holidays. The hours at times were unbearably long. This is not to say that servants were treated unkindly: rather that for their slender wages, paid quarterly, their employers had serious expectations.

Sometimes there were quite unrealistic demands made upon servants. John Coker Egerton, the Sussex writer, tells of a conversation he had with an old woman who looked back over fifty years to the 1830s when she worked on a Sussex farm. She told him:

> "I'd be churning twice a week and cheesing twice a week and brewing twice, besides washing and baking; and six cows to milk every night and morning, and sometimes a dozen pigs to feed. There were four men lived in the house and I'd all the boilin' to do - the cabbage and peas and pork for their dinners - besides all the beds to make; and sometimes I did make 'em in a fashion, that's certain! One morning, I mind, I got up at four and worked till twelve at night, and the missus wanted me to pick a couple of ducks.
>
> 'No, missus,' I says. 'I really can't; I be quite tired.'
>
> 'Tired?' says she. 'If I was a young woman like you I should be ashamed of myself.'
>
> Ah! it just was a treat to get an hour or two to one's

self of a Sunday! I was twelve years a servant at 1s 6d a week, and then I got married; and when my husband died I went to service again, and for all I'd been a married woman, I only got 1s 6d. After a while I got 2s a week, and then a man who'd been a soldier wanted somebody as could keep house for him, and he gave me 2s 6d a week.

Mercy, the gals nowadays don't know naun about work."

The girls who went out to work in private houses had a different kind of experience from those on many farms. Jane Burgess, a 12 year old, working for Mrs Brook, and Sarah Reed, employed by the Kings, would also have experiences different from the girls who worked for the families of John and George Woodhams. The former, a maltster, had six boys and girls aged between ten and twenty, whilst his relative had six children below seven years of age. Charlotte Goldsmith, registered as a nurse in the house of Mrs Sarah Simmonds, an elderly lady of independent means, doubtless had different requirements imposed on her.

Several tradesmen including Brooker the tanner; Bridger, grocer/ draper/undertaker; Hastings, plumber/glazier/painter as well as being mine host at 'The George', had female servants, most of them in their teens. Advertisements of the time suggested that applications from women over the age of twenty-two would be unwelcome. This is understandable for these were live-in posts and 'hangers-on' were often a nuisance.

In 1841 three housekeepers were recorded, all of them over fifty years of age. In North Street Jane Miller acted as housekeeper for Ann Collins and two men; also in the same street, at a house now divided into two (Little Dene and The Dene), Mrs Stace was identified as housekeeper to her husband and James Woodhams, both of the men being millers. Another lady looked after Alfred Godden the butcher and his apprentice in his home in the High Street (Clifton House).

What is not known is the number of women working as servants on a daily basis, some of them as cooks, others as charladies, or most usually doing general work. The absence of such information makes it impossible to calculate either the total numbers so employed and the precise nature of work being done. It seems reasonable to suggest, for example, that the tailor, Charles

Shelly and his wife, with a large family ranging in age from three to twenty years of age, as well as an apprentice living in, had a daily servant but there is no available evidence.

The domestic education which girls in service received in these situations ultimately did much to improve overall standards of housekeeping. Generally speaking, life in service did much for many girls. Some of the kinds of skills which they learnt are described by Ellman:

> "If there was no housekeeper, the mistress superintended her maid in the making of pickles, jams, wines, sauces, sweets, etc. Home-made medicines were in common use and every mistress of a household would produce them as a matter of course. All the needlework was done at home by hand, not machine, and the ladies of the family would work elaborate pieces of dainty needlework."

If service at times resulted in the assumption of gross snobbishness or prissy refinement on the part of some, for the most part the influences of life in service were beneficial to girls as eventual managers of their own homes.

FARMING

In the period this account treats of, agriculture was Britain's principal industry. By 1840 it still accounted for nearly one third of the national income and engaged something in the order of two million people as employees. The long-past wars had produced enormous profits and even the slow deflationary descent which followed for nearly twenty years, even the bad harvests which accompanied that decline, did not prevent farmers from accumulating more and more wealth. By 1837, they had reached the dawn of a new 'Golden Age'.

The other industries which had prospered in the war - brickmaking, brewing, leather - were less fortunate. The militia men billeted locally had had their barracks tiled and repaired; they had drunk the local beer in vast quantities; they had ordered leather gloves and contracted for gaiters. The shops flourished with a captive clientele. The soldiery was present in great enough numbers, and over a long enough period, to have contributed to the making of some modest fortunes. Sufficient money was made by some local people to engage in property speculation. Several of the tradesmen ended the war owning more than one village house. The tanner, Charles Brooker, owned thirteen; Richard Haryott and John Hilton, both shoemakers, were house owners; William Kidd, the saddler, owned several patches of land on which to keep a few sheep and pigs, cattle and horses.

But the labourer, whether he worked on a farm or the roads or in one of the small industries, had no share in this. His standard of living, comfortable enough, all things considered, began to decline at the end of the eighteenth century, and was to continue to do even more so when the bad times came. And the bad times came when the war ended and the soldiers left. By the time Victoria came to the throne in 1837 many labourers were pauperised. Brewing to any important extent was over; brickmaking had long gone; the tannery would survive another half dozen years.

The larger tenant farmers, however, had enjoyed huge profits during the war. Now, despite a prolonged deflationary period, they had managed to more than survive. Indeed, thanks to the Government's protective policies, as well as their own careful management of their farms, they were wealthy. And not only wealthy, it seems. They were different from farmers in times past. They had begun to set themselves up in rather grander fashion than their predecessors. Now they were not content to call themselves farmers: they appear in the local baptismal registers as 'yeoman' or 'gentleman'. Their homes were finer than before. At Burnt House, Charles Springate Brooker had a governess for his three younger daughters as well as a cook and house servants. He was not alone in this. More and more farmers had indoor staff. Over at Clapham House, Litlington, the landowning Reverend Thomas Scutt had a very grand household, employing a staff of four female and three male servants both from his village and from Alfriston. There are many references at the time to what might now be called conspicuous consumption. Farmers were buying finer clothes, gigs and phaetons for their wives and daughters. They were building fine houses to replace the old buildings of former times. Increasingly they were to demonstrate a greater reluctance to work and eat side by side with their men.

In 1843, a versifier looked upon the changes with a more than jaundiced eye.

Old Style
Man, to the plough,
Wife, to the cow,
Girl, to the yarn,
Boy, to the barn
And your rent will be netted.

New Style
Man, tally-ho,
Miss, piano,
Wife, silk and satin,
Boy, Greek and Latin,
And you'll all be gazetted.

The four principal farms in the parish were all tenanted on seven year leases. At Frog Firle, Henry Pagden had held the lease from 1816 and he was to continue as the Earl of Burlington's tenant until 1860. At the neighbouring farm, Burnt House, William Roods was the tenant of General Chowne before handing over the lease to Charles Springate Brooker in 1844. Winton Farm was leased in turn from Lord Gage by William Jenner, John King, and Edward Cane. King moved from this farm to Berwick Court, just beyond the parish boundary, in 1842. The Dray family had for many years been the tenants of Thomas Shain Carter at Deans Place until Peter Pagden took over in 1842, although his tenancy was curtailed in 1845.

An incidental curiosity - Deans Place was taxed as two farms, the second being called Town Farm and this ran across the Tye and along the water meadows as far as Longbridge.

The only other farm of consequence was William Madgwick's 180 acres of downland where he pastured sheep, presumably in considerable numbers. Additionally, artisans, shopkeepers and some of the wealthier tradesmen either rented or even owned pieces of land as pasturage or orchards, for as yet not every Englishman had been wrenched from his rural birthright.

The farms in the Cuckmere Valley were in the main larger than most in the country. Here, the wealthy tenant farmers, having survived the depression which had gripped Britain since the end of the war, could, if they wished, afford to experiment and it was this along with their more efficient organisation which enabled them to prosper when many smaller farms were going to the wall. Market forces favoured the strong and the energetic: they more than weathered the worst.

At the time, a farm of average size was something in the order of 110 acres. At Winton Street, there were 454 acres of arable and pasture; at Deans Place, 697 acres; Henry Pagden farmed 510 acres at Frog Firle whilst at Burnt House there were 443 acres. The parishes of Berwick, Lullington and Litlington and the hamlet of Milton Street accounted for another 3,000 acres of farmland.

Farms of such size required considerable annual investment. Two examples will suggest the scale in the 1840s. At Berwick Court, just a few hundred yards outside the parish boundaries, there was a farm of 370 acres. Here, there were a flock of 870 pure bred Southdown sheep, 120 cattle and 20 cart horses.

In the 'Sussex Agricultural Express' an inventory of farm equipment at Deans Place itemises the following:

"3 excellent broad wheel waggons, 9 narrow wheel ditto, 5 good dung carts, 2 light carts, 6 strong Sussex wheel ploughs, 2 sets of harrows, a land roller, a famous corn cracker, winnowing and seed sowing machines, a nearly new set of harness, ox yokes and chains, plough harness, 3 iron hog troughs, and the usual small farming implements."

In addition to cattle, pigs and horses, many of the farmers in Alfriston and the neighbouring parishes had up to twenty oxen purely for draught purposes and others, their work days over, being fattened up for market. The farmers liked their oxen for despite their requiring at least a man and a boy to manage them as a team, they were cheap to shoe, feed and harness. Best of all, from the farmers' point of view, at the end of their lives, their carcasses brought money at the slaughterhouse.

For a farmer to run a farm of 500 acres at this time the expenses have been estimated at £5,000 per annum. There were wages to be paid, land tax, tithe, purchase of new stock and equipment and maintenance of old equipment. The Poor Rate alone cost about £200 each year, even if many farmers manipulated this to their own advantage.

After the war, when corn prices fell, the landed interest, accustomed to the benefits of their war-time monopoly and fearing cheap corn imports from Europe and America, were supported by successive Governments whose Corn Laws made it less profitable for foreigners to sell the corn here. In spite of its not being great corn country because of its chalky soil, considerable quantities of corn were grown in Sussex and the security of its farmers ensured.

The farmers were saved: the labourers were not. The southern English labourers on poor wages, resulting in part from a peace-time labour surplus, lost their cheap white loaf, that symbol of their superiority over porridge-eating Scots and potato-guzzling Irish. So, whilst the poor were counselled on the virtues of frugality, of the nutritious qualities of the cheap potato, sago and rice, the farmers were protected against any harsh economic conditions. This further distanced them from their workers. In earlier centuries, they had all slept under the same roof, eaten at the same board: now, it was cheaper to let the labourers rent their own homes, buy their own food. Paying money wages separated farmer and labourer in a way unknown to previous generations. The census shows a few families living in farm cottages. Whilst their particular tasks are not identified, the men were generally prized specialist workers - ploughmen, hedgers and ditchers, cow keepers. The rest found their rented accommodation where they could.

In the interests of fairness, however, it ought to be said that not all farm workers had enjoyed being housed and fed by their masters. John Coker Egerton quotes a verse which amply demonstrates this:

"Pork and cabbage all the year
Mouldy bread and sour beer
Rusty bacon, stinking cheese
A chaff bed full of fleas -
Who do you think would live here?"

Certainly in the good times the labourer's expectations had been higher than this. In the bad days, he would not have complained at being once more under his master's roof.

SHEEP AND SHEPHERDS

If the chalky downland soil did not produce the finest corn, it served as a wonderful base for sheep. This had always been the case but the scrawny animl of earlier times had been developed into a larger, fleshier animal. At Glynde, from the previous century, imbued with an energetic and sustained passion for scientific farming, the Ellman family had improved cattle and had experimented with root crops and winter feed. Their great triumph, however, was the Southdown Sheep, a new model animal, a hardy beast, systematically bred to produce excellent meat and good wool. Now, with the greater development of root crops - turnips, mangolds - the sheep could be fed in part on the arable in both summer and winter. Here, they manured the ground to an astonishing richness and the consequent corn yields were yet greater. One could almost recite a mantra, descriptive of an endless cycle: roots and sheep and plough and sheep and drill and sow and corn and harvest and roots and sheep .....

SOUTH DOWN EWE.
Bred by Mr. Ellman of Glynd Sussex.

Ultimately, the sheep were destined for the markets at Lewes or Hailsham or even Smithfield but there were annual visits of the shearing gangs. Each year upwards of fifteen men and boys would descend perhaps on Deans Place, then move on up to Burnt House, their captain, in his gold braided cap, fixing the contract with the farmer and then directing the whole enterprise. His team members, sustained each day by mugs of 'swanky', the mildest of beers, or 'stokos', a lemon-flavoured oatmeal drink, would each reckon to shear up to forty animals a day. And if in their haste they nicked the flesh, the tar boy, his brush in hand, would be at the ready to dab at the injured part.

When all was complete, the wool packed and ready for a visiting wool factor or for the carrier, the team would move on to other valley farms. In its turn, the wool would make for other markets or for the railway en route for the northern mills.

An idea of numbers? Back in 1801, on Alfriston's farms there were about 1,450 ewes and 270 lambs. The parishes of Berwick, Litlington and Lullington accounted at this time for another 2,000 sheep. It is said that there were 200,000 sheep in a six mile swathe from coast to downland in the thirty-three miles between Steyning and Eastbourne. In 1841 at Berwick Court, on his 370 acres, John King had 820 sheep.

But enough of numbers. Perhaps we merely need to know that our heavenly hills, had we raised our eyes to them, were speckled with sheep, great constellations of them, almost wherever we cared to look.

Of the men who cared for them, much has been written of their independent cast of mind, of their concern for their flocks, their pride in their work, their skill. They seem romantic figures, these downland shepherds. We think of them outlined against dawn skies, their heavy white wool overcoats covering their workday smocks, their corduroy pants and sheepskin gaiters. Sometimes they wear dog-hair hats, hard enough to stand on, or straw hats which they have painted lead grey to keep out the wet. Some prefer top hats or billy cocks. On their way to the slopes in the morning, picking their way up the track from Winton or Frog Firle, with the flock they have collected from the fold in the arable, the shepherds carry their wide umbrellas in case the weather should change. The plaited frail, in which they pack their bread and cheese and the variety of small tools they may need, is slung across their shoulders. The crook they carry is unlikely to be their best one. This, especially if it should come from Pyecombe, they take out only for visits to the big fairs and markets, for Lewes and

Hailsham or even further afield. They are for show, these crooks, not work; they are for Sunday best.

At lambing time, the shepherds bring their flocks down to the farm, erecting wattle fences in the yard for the ewes and their new-born. The men themselves stay in an outhouse close at hand or in a hut on wheels, not altogether unlike those they might have seen or heard of on Brighton's beaches. In cold or rain, in snow or biting wind, often by the dim light of a horn lamp, they deliver the young.

Nor should it be thought that this is the only busy time in the shepherds' calendar. Nursing the flock, moving it on, eyeing it always, mending, planning, that is the shepherds' day. They need to repair folds and canister bells; fleeces are to be trimmed; skin eaten by parasites has to be soothed with some or other home-made cure. They pass on their nostrums for the variety of ailments to which sheep are prone, telling the teg-boy how a mix of blue vitriol and boiled vinegar is the answer to a mild dose of foot and mouth. There are other home-made preparations too - mallow and flannel leaf, just the thing for coughs or the gripes. Or there's Jack-in-the-Hedge - red campion leaves - the ideal remedy for sore and infected places.

These cures would be well enough known to Thomas Tucknott, the Winton Street shepherd. John Levett over at Frog Firle would know them too, for they were handed down over long generations, refined, the amounts altered slightly in the light of preference and experience. Benjamin Russell, William Tripper, Henry Breach, three other Alfriston shepherds, would also share this knowledge. It is extremely likely that some of the village boys worked with the shepherds although only Breach had sons to follow on. But with most farms having at least 300 or 400 sheep - and bear in mind John King's 820 animals on one of the smaller local farms - there would be need of additional help. Although there were men who at times looked after as many as 900 sheep without assistance, these were rare.

Most trades have their lore and language, their particular ways of naming, their indicators of professional exclusivity. It is not a feature unique to shepherds. Yet their counting systems throughout Britain, all of similar pattern yet all different, offer a particular curiosity to the outsider. At the day's end when the shepherd and his teg-boy had brought down the flock, they counted the sheep into the fold in pairs, using the old Sussex shepherd's chant.

"Wintherum, wontherum,
Twintherum, twontherum,
Wagtail.

Whitebelly, corum,
Dar, diddle,
Den.

Etherum, atherum,
Shootherum, cootherum,
Windbar.

Bobtail, inadik,
Dyadik, burpit,
Ecack,
Tally."

And so with that shout of "Tally", the first forty animals would be counted into the fold.

What to make of this? Nothing, save perhaps that it seems to proclaim that there were mysteries here to be learnt slowly, along with the other arts and skills of one of the oldest trades. Of all the farm workers, the shepherd was perhaps the one most highly regarded. He was the man who was never laid-off, never put on short-time, never sent home because the weather was so bad that his labour was not required. In drought and flood, he was there each day. Whatever the state of the industry, he was expected to work. Let corn fail or let it flourish, let there be blight on the root crops or let them prosper, this was immaterial. The shepherd worked throughout the year, every day. No day for him was a holiday.

In recompense for his hard working conditions, seven days a week, in sun and wind, hail, ice and snow, the shepherd earned perhaps 14s, perhaps more. Certainly he took home more than his neighbour, the ordinary farm labourer. At Christmas time, his employer might even give him a leg of beef. In 1841, it might be that the shepherds were less well off than their predecessors in the days of the old tenantry flocks. In the previous century, when they had cared for mixed flocks, the sheep of several farmers, shepherds had often received two or three ewes as a bonus at the season's end. The consequence was that some of these shepherds had ended their days quite comfortably with flocks of their own or a cottage with a garden as well as a sizeable sum of money. Enclosure had put an end to such largesse from the owners. Nevertheless, of all the workers, the downland shepherd remained the most highly prized.

SOUTH DOWN RAM, *bred by Mr Ellman of GLYND, SUSSEX.*

But on the lonely windswept tops, when they were out tending sheep, when they were not nursing the sick or watching out for stray dogs or sheep stealers, there was always some associated task. Or possibly they read their books. John Dudeney, who married an Alfriston girl, had taught himself enough to set up a Mechanics Institute with the scholarly Mark Anthony Lower. Others too used their time profitably enough, catching rabbits or wheatears or corncrakes or making tallow candles from the fat in the sheep's tails.

They were an exclusive race, a group of men who despite the ties of their work were the freest of the men on the land.

SOME SMALL INDUSTRIES

Perhaps this title ought to have included the word 'services'. I can think of no other word but a service to indicate what it was that Elizabeth Hasting, a 60 year old widow, provided. She is described as a mangler. This was of course not an uncommon means of earning money - rashly, I was on the point of writing 'making a living', but that would seem an overstatement. Among the poorest people and not just in rural areas, it was customary to hire the use of a mangle for a small sum of money, say, 1d. In Alfriston, the wet clothes would be taken to Mrs Hasting's cottage and either she would mangle the clothes or those who had brought them to her would be allowed to use the machine. At the end of the last century, there was still a mangler in the village.

Two other women, 65 year old Elizabeth Haryott and her daughter Susan (40), were laundresses. Whether they went out to houses or whether the clothing was brought to them cannot be known but it is possible that they too possessed a mangle which could be hired. If these ladies visited the more substantial houses, it is probable that the clothes were aired in the warmth of the large kitchens. The Haryott ladies, although there is no indication of where they lived, would have neither space nor kindling enough to dry off great amounts of laundry in the cottage in which they presumably lived.

Because the census of 1841 requires the occupation of the head of house only, we are denied information about the work of many women. It is not sufficient to assume them to be housewives. Many of them were involved in either full- or part-time labours. Some of them are likely to have made articles of straw. For example, the frails, those all purpose bags which shepherds slung over their shoulders, were usually made of plaited straw. Whilst the saddler John Durrant listed frail making among his accomplishments it is likely that the work was tendered out to women in the village. Only one woman is known to have been occupied as a straw hat maker, though others are likely to have been so employed. Broad brimmed hats for women working in the fields were of course essential if they were to maintain the same pale complexion as the respectable ladies of the parish.

Closely allied to the above craft is basketmaking. A photograph of 1927 shows a group of nine men and women from Alfriston over the caption 'Basketmakers'. There was, however, no one in the 1841 census of the parish so described. It might be that some wives were involved in the work but it was not exclusively a woman's trade. Basket making was, of course, a truly country craft, using easily available local materials. Thomas Geering refers to 'Old Twigs' Levett and the Arlington census confirms that two Levetts, Joseph and Richard, were basketmakers. There is little doubt that their families - between them, Joseph and Richard could muster two wives and four children aged between 9 and 20 - were part of this venture. They appear to have worked in an outhouse at Milton Street. The withies from which they made their baskets came from the trees which lined the river. We are reminded of these today by the Willows Car Park. Other sources of willow rods, however, might have been on two Berwick farms. Two fields - Quinnyers at Church Farm and another at Berwick Court - are particularly mentioned as growing osiers in the register accompanying the Tithe Map.

The Levetts made articles for a variety of purposes. They provided baskets for seed sowers, stone pickers and lobster catchers. They produced intricate bird cages, for the Victorians loved a linnet or a canary in the house. As a side-line, the Levetts caught eels in the Cuckmere in the eel-hives for which they were well-known. After they were skinned, weighed and bunched, the eels were brought to customers in Alfriston or sent on to Eastbourne. The eel skins were sold separately to the fellmongery where, after treatment, they were used to tie together the two lengths of wood that made up a flail.

Basketmaking was a typical cottage industry. It required small outlay, no expensive materials or equipment, a specific skill and a ready market. The Levetts seem to have had all of these.

In Lullington lived Dame Hill. She ought not to be ignored for although like the Levetts she was not of Alfriston she was close enough to consider the village her principal market. In addition, she is chosen as a representative of a skill which might well have been employed by some other women in Alfriston parish even though the census offers no examples. Dame Hill was a mop maker. She collected pieces of wool which she cleaned and carded and then spun into rats' tails. She then fashioned them into mop heads.

It is unfortunate that so little hard evidence exists descriptive of local cottage industries. That many widows, mothers, wives and daughters needed to work is indisputable. Many of them would be involved in charring or in service as 'dailies' but many others worked on a seasonal or part-time basis in certain of the small industries - gloving, straw trades, basketmaking, mop making, and perhaps other unspecified manufactures.

THE SHOPKEEPERS

In 1840 there were as many shops and traders in Alfriston as there are today. There were two grocers, two butchers, a draper, a baker as well as a tailor, a dressmaker, a milliner and a straw hat maker. In addition, there was an undertaking service provided by Bridger the grocer. It does seem surprising that in a period of such poverty such a variety of shops should be in evidence. Perhaps today we should not so readily recognise them as shops. There were few window displays and inside, goods were often ranged on shelves behind the serving counter or hidden away in labelled drawers. Nor was there any clear-cut arrangement among the shopkeepers and tradesmen concerning what they sold. There were instances of saddlers selling eggs, butchers greens and dairy produce, grocers selling anything save meat. There was a whole range of goods which might have been sold from the shelves of any of the shopkeepers or even from the workshops of some of the artisans. The grocer or the saddler, the draper or blacksmith even, might have offered nails, tools, brushes, pegs, garden seeds, black lead, twine, cord, starch, soda, whiting, sandpaper, bath brick, Fuller's earth, soap.

George Bodle and his wife, an elderly couple, were grocers, perhaps in a small way. There is no indication of where they conducted their business but in one document there is a reference to shops in Star Lane. A possible location, therefore, might be opposite the present garage. Blocked up doors and windows hint at a house here which might conceivably have been the Bodle's shop.

William Bridger's shop (Tudor Cafe) in the High Street was successful enough for him to support a wife, a 10 year old son, Frederick, and an infant, Henry. The business was large enough to warrant the engagement of George Russell as his apprentice as well as a female servant. Here, Bridger would teach young Russell about choosing and blending tea, roasting and grinding coffee, mixing herbs, curing bacon, washing and drying cut fruit and all the other skills of grocery work.

At this period, there were regular complaints about the prices charged in village shops. It was this which made them near inaccessible to many poor. Even though credit was often available in some shops for as long as a year, many of the goods were beyond the purses of the poor who, when they could, purchased many of their wants from either the tallyman or a visiting packman. But for Bridger the grocer there was another clientele, altogether more substantial, with distinctly richer tastes. None of the other villages, of course, with one exception, boasted a grocer's shop. At Berwick, the wife of one of the small farmers claimed to be a shopkeeper but her resources were slim, scant opposition for Bridger to whom daintier palates would turn when they did not pick up their purchases in Hailsham or Lewes. To some extent farmers could satisfy many of their own needs but the Sangers and Cooleys, the Brookers and Marchants, the almost carriage trade, doubtless bought many of their requirements locally. It is likely that Bridger delivered too. Whilst he might not be enthusiastic enough to negotiate Hindover - in the 1930s, motor car owners were warned of its demands - other roads were passable in most seasons, save when there were floods. He could cross Longbridge and take his goods into Litlington and Lullington and Milton Street.

The butcher, Alfred Godden, lived in the High Street (Clifton House). In the garden behind the house is a small brick building which in its time served as a domestic malthouse and later as a shoemaker's workshop. The apportionment register refers to this building as a shop. Was it, one wonders, Godden's butcher shop? If so, it could be approached down the narrow twitten between the present Grenville House and Manor House.

William Banks ran both his meal business and his butchery in Market Cross House (Smugglers Inn). The present bar still has meat hooks in evidence and at the rear is the slaughterhouse Stanton Collins had built in 1826.

Two butchers? Who ate all this meat? Cobbett wrote that the Sussex labourer would insist on meat pudding as part of his diet. Of course he would, but only when he could afford it. Elsewhere we learn that pork, often raised at home, rather than beef or lamb, was his favourite. But butcher's shop prices, like grocer's prices, were usually too high for the poor rural worker. Even the charming vicar of Berwick, Edward Ellman, claimed that he could rarely afford meat. Whilst this takes some believing, it may serve to indicate the fact that Ellman regarded meat as relatively expensive. So then, who favoured Godden and Banks with their orders? Thirty years earlier local butchers had done well enough with soldiers stationed at Winton and in the village itself. But the departure of the military had robbed the village of a significant purchasing power. It was not as if after 1834 the parish had a large Union workhouse which might have contracted with the butchers for meat. Cobbett had, of course, always declared that soldiers and workhouse inmates were better fed than the labouring poor.

At the end of the preceding century, the "jernal" of John Burgess, a not especially successful fellmonger at Ditchling, records the dishes he enjoyed over the years and serves as an example of the difference in living standards between men of his station and the abject poor. Even this modest tradesman was acquainted with beef pudding, hog meat chine, spare rib, veal pudding, roast goose, rabbit pudding, leg of mutton, ham, leg of beef, pork, fowl pie, plum pudding, gingerbread, apple and damson pie, wine, beer, punch and tea. The artisans and tradesmen, it seems, continued to live relatively well even in straitened times. It was the labouring poor who rarely enjoyed such fare.

Perhaps the vast quantities guzzled by the wealthy and even the better-off artisans in the previous century were toned down by the early Victorian period, but there were still some good trenchermen about. We know that from details of the Subscription Dinners and Benefit Society Dinners during this period. So did Alfriston's middle classes, superior tradesmen and artisans provide sufficient number of customers to warrant two butchers? Surprisingly enough, it must seem so.

Charles Shelly, the tailor, stocked ready-made clothing to answer the needs of most levels of Alfriston's society. He also made clothes to measure. Working in the shop with their father were Shelly's sons, Walter and Charles, as well as young Reuben Cox, the apprentice from Longbridge. It is more than probable that Shelly's daughters, Mary Ann and Elizabeth, were called upon to work there too, either at the tailoring or behind the counter. Perhaps they did minor repairs. No doubt Mrs Shelly's hands were full enough with 9 year old Francis, Owen aged 6 and Edgar the baby, to allow her much time to work in the shop. The precise location of Shelly's house and shop is unknown but there is a tentative reference to his living in one of the High Street cottages (Steamer Cottages).

Was there really enough tailoring to maintain such a large

family? Presumably so. Shelly would keep some stock of heavy shirts and corduroy clothing for the labourers, although they often purchased from travelling packmen. Perhaps for Alfriston's aristocracy - the Brookers, the Pagdens - there was a small range of frock coats, dark trousers, frilled shirts, fancy waistcoats, cravats and overcoats, as well as decently thick underpants and vests to keep out the valley's damp winter chill. And hats, of course, for all occasions.

The clergy - Scutt and Bohun Smith over at Litlington, Ellman at Berwick - might not have patronised the village tailor. They would more probably plump for the wider and more substantial selections of Lewes where so many absentee clergy lived and where good class shops existed to satisfy their needs.

It would be surprising if Charles Shelly did not keep some stock of work dresses, shawls and blouses. There would be aprons, too, worn every day, and without which the Victorian working woman felt incomplete. Older women doubtless still adopted the old-fashioned caps which tied under the chin and all, irrespective of age, would need protective bonnets, for who would wish her sunburnt face to announce her base origins? It is presumed that Charles Shelly took care of such demands. Perhaps he might even keep other garments more suitable for the Pagden ladies and vicars' wives, something appropriate for morning or evening wear or afternoon visiting. The roughness was wearing off after all. The polite rituals of the last century, those Austen-like courtesies, the visiting card, the taking of tea, the little soirées, must have transferred by now to rural Sussex. Of course, it is known that some ladies, the more comfortably off, were taking themselves to Brighton. There, of course, once the railway line was completed, once there was a station at Berwick, all sorts of possibilities opened up.

Ladies had yet another alternative. They could call on Maria Geering, the dressmaker in Weavers Lane. Sarah Haryott, a 15 year old, was also a dressmaker and it is likely that she worked alongside Mrs Geering. Then there were the milliners, Mrs Winch and Mrs Ridgway, capable of making hats for afternoon tea.

It must be asked what range of materials, what frequency of custom there was, which enabled George Woodhams, not yet 30 years old, and with a wife and six children, not one above the age of 7, to employ two apprentices, Henry Peerless and young Richard

Haryott. And in addition there was his servant, the resonantly named Harriet Haryott. Certainly Woodhams was comfortably off. Although he rented his house, shop, barn and yard (The Paint Shop) in the High Street, he was the owner of two other houses, one in West Street, the other in the High Street, both of which properties he rented out.

And was there so much in drapery? Reports on the condition of labourers' cottages were mixed although some were described as clean, simply furnished and well curtained. Even so, no cottager's wife was in any position to renew her curtains with any regularity. Furthermore, in such a numerous dissenting community, in which so many tradesmen, including George Woodhams, were chapel-goers, the village resonated with notions of thrift and modesty. It was not in keeping with the Non-conformist view of the world, irrespective of how much a family earned, to go in for excessive expenditure or conspicuous display.

Nevertheless by the 1840s it was in the power of George Woodhams to offer to Alfriston the riches of the Lancashire factories. Now, machine-made articles were readily available and in such quantity and variety as hitherto unknown. Now, there was a whole wealth of table runners, mantelpiece decorations, table-leg covers, curtains; and an unheard of range of cotton and woollen items, a choice unsuspected only a few years earlier. Any self-respecting draper could now offer materials with which to make items of clothing, shirts, vests, petticoats, nightgowns, as well as pillow cases and mattress covers. Did he do so? Could he compete with Eastbourne and Brighton, with Hailsham and Lewes? Did he have a large and loyal enough clientele to accept what it was in his power to offer them? Or did he discover that drapery did not pay? After the death of Charles Brooker in 1843, Woodhams took over the fellmongery for a time. By 1845, he was describing himself as a glover, a natural enough progression for a man owning a fellmongery, although it is not to be supposed that he made the gloves himself. In the same year, he also proclaimed himself a grocer, his shop presumably selling dried fruits alongside shirt lengths, pounds of tea next to mattress ticking, ham by the pairs of gloves.

What did it all come to? Impossible to say. But within a few years, the family emigrated to the United States.

The last of the shopkeepers in this little list is Richard

Haryott who makes his appearance in 1841 as a shoemaker. In the baptismal register of 1843, he announces himself as a baker. Of course, he was juggling both occupations and seemingly with success. One of his sons was a shoemaker, another a baker. In the bakery there was an apprentice. Whether Richard Haryott was a master baker or a master shoemaker cannot be ascertained; what is apparent is that he and his descendants went on down the years turning out loaves from the same North Street house (Badgers) and that at the same address he went on making shoes.

These small shopkeepers were comfortable enough. Several of them owned their own houses; some owned more than one. They were thrifty and ambitious, yet it does surprise one to read how frequently they strayed into selling articles stocked by their competitors. It does seem that they must also have been a close knit group. Most of them were members of the chapel. Perhaps it was here they learnt to tolerate each other's intrusive stocks of materials.

APPRENTICES

Several of the artisans and shopkeepers had taken on apprentices. Reuben Page worked with Robert Wilson the bricklayer; Henry Peerless with George Woodhams the draper; Fred Carter with the baker, Richard Haryott. Other boys and young men were apprenticed to the cooper, the saddler, the tailor, the butcher, the builder.

William Bridger's apprentice, George Russell, worked in the High Street grocery (Tudor Cafe). As Bridger's business was not confined to groceries but also took in his drapery and undertaking businesses we may assume that young George's training embraced each of these areas. He would, however, have been taken on to learn one trade in particular and his indentures would specify which branch of his master's business he was to learn about. The census specifically identifies George as a grocer's apprentice and it was this trade which his master was obliged to teach him. In the larger towns and cities, there was at this time a quite considerable change going forward in shops of this kind. At last, goods were being displayed and masters were now tending to neglect the training in the preparation of teas, coffees, meats and so on, in favour of emphasising more positively the apprentice's role as a salesman behind the counter. Perhaps in Alfriston, however, the old ways still held, more attention being paid to those other behind-the-scenes aspects of the work.

Reuben Cox, apprentice to Charles Shelly, the tailor, doubtless received a traditional apprenticeship, learning all the aspects of measuring, cutting out, sewing and altering, which was the staple of the work. At some point, later in the century, there would be machines to do much of the work in so much shorter time but, until then, the trade which Charles Shelly was teaching Reuben Cox continued as it had for hundreds of years.

What made the apprenticeship special of course was the two-way agreement made by master and apprentice. This is an intrinsic feature of apprenticeship indentures in which there is a high value placed upon morality, straight dealing, loyalty. It is simple to dismiss these documents as so much out-dated cant, especially when it is evident that the indenture document has been purchased off the peg. But the success of the apprenticeship, the fact that a man so often remained loyal to his master, that he carried on the work, the same business often, suggests that it was a bond entered into with high seriousness.

An announcement in the 'Sussex Agricultural Express' in 1840 is not untypical. It is addressed to "Saddlers and Harness Makers" by a father seeking to place his son "as an apprentice, where he may be treated as one of the family, and have attention paid to his morals, as well as to obtain a thorough knowledge of the above business". How clearly this exemplifies the expected relationship between master and man.

John Durrant's indenture offers a good insight into the arrangement that he, his father and his future employer, the saddler, William Marchant, entered into in 1829. They put their names to a scheme not solely of a long term of training but also of welfare and mutual fair dealing. It may be easy to scoff at some of the prohibitions within the document: it is less easy to dismiss the sentiment and intention behind it.

> "This Indenture Witnesseth that John Durrant by and with the consent and approbation of his Father Caleb Durrant of Saddlescombe in the County of Sussex servant testified by his executing these presents doth put himself Apprentice to William Marchant of Alfriston in the said county saddler and harness maker to learn his Art and with him after the Manner of an Apprentice to serve from the Eighteenth day of March instant unto the full End and Term of seven years and a quarter of another year from thence next following to be fully complete and ended During which term the said Apprentice his Master faithfully shall serve his secrets keep his lawful commands everywhere gladly do he shall do no damage to his said Master nor see to be done of others but to his Power shall tell or forthwith give warning to his said Master of the same he shall not waste the Goods of his said Master nor lend them unlawfully to any he shall not commit fornication nor contract Matrimony within the said Term he shall not play Cards or Dice Tables or any other unlawful Games whereby his said Master may have any loss with his own

goods or others during the said Term without licence of his said Master he shall neither buy nor sell he shall not haunt Taverns or Playhouses nor absent himself from his said Master's service day or night unlawfully But in all things as a faithful Apprentice he shall behave himself towards his said Master and all his during the said Term and the said William Marchant in consideration of the sum of Twenty One pounds sterling to him in hand paid by the said Caleb Durrant at or before the Execution of these presents The Receipt whereof is hereby acknowledged and of the further sum of Twenty One pounds sterling to be paid to him the said William Marchant by the said Caleb Durrant on the Eighteenth day of November One thousand eight hundred and thirty two said Apprentice in the Art of a Saddler and Harness Maker which he useth by the best means that he can shall teach and Instruct or cause to be taught and instructed Finding unto the said Apprentice Sufficient Meat Drink and Lodging and all other Necessaries during the said Term and the said Caleb Durrant for himself his Heirs Executors and Administrators doth hereby covenant and agree to and with the said William Marchant in manner following that is to say To pay unto the said William Marchant the said further sum of Twenty One pounds sterling at the time herein before mentioned and also to find and provide for the said Apprentice proper and sufficient cloaths washing mending and all other necessaries during the said Term.

And for the true performance of all and every the said Covenants and Agreements either of the said Parties bindeth himself unto the other by these Presents In Witness whereof the Parties above named to these Indentures have put their Hands and Seals the thirteenth day of March and in the tenth year of the Reign of our Sovereign Lord George the Fourth by the Grace of God of the United Kingdom of Great Britain and Ireland King Defender of the Faith and in the Year of our Lord One Thousand Eight Hundred and twenty nine.

(Signed) John Durrant, Caleb Durrant,
Will[m] Marchant"

John Durrant from Saddlescombe qualified as a saddler with William Marchant in 1836. There is every reason to believe that he was successful in his work for, in 1849, he is listed as a member of the Parish Vestry. By 1851, he had married Ann Haryott of Alfriston and was employing a girl as a nurse for his one year old baby. His regular listing in Kelly's Directory suggests that he was self-employed. He was still working as a saddler in the 1870s and lived until 1897.

The two factors which stand out from the Burial Registers are that so many people lived into their 70s and 80s and that at the other end of the scale so many children and infants died.

Nearly every year saw the death of some man or woman, old even by present expectations. In 1826, for example, of the fifteen deaths, four were of people aged between 70 and 84. In 1835, of the four deaths recorded, two were 73 year olds and a third, an 85 year old. In 1844, of the ten who died, four were aged 78, 84, 87 and 88. The conclusion to be drawn is not that everyone lived to a ripe old age but that, contrary to our preconceived notions, a quite surprising number did so.

Many children died in their earliest years and the deaths of others, well into adolescence, are recorded too. The Wilsons in the High Street outlived all their six children, none of whom lived beyond 23 years, and three of whom, Ann (12), Mary (4) and Sally (11) died within eighteen months of each other in 1843 and 1844. In 1849, there were the deaths of Walter Reed, an infant, John Pettit (4), Esther Hilton (5), Henrietta Godden (5), Emma Marchant (3). I name these children because they are somehow familiar to me; their parents, their brothers and sisters, are recorded elsewhere in this account.

Down the years there is a depressing toll of children and young boys and girls who never reach maturity. There are the deaths of tenant farmers' sons like James Dray at 14, Peter Pagden aged 2, and the 15 week old Henry Brooker at Burnt House, all three deaths, proof if it were needed, that the wealthy were not spared anguish. George Carrick the glover loses a 3 year old child and there is the death of Emma Levett, only 18 months. In the Registers we read of the death of babies only days old. Somehow we cannot imagine it, the loss, so regular, so feared, five or six young ones some years. What griefs they bore, these fathers and mothers. What griefs they must have anticipated throughout their days, knowing the high chance of losing some of their babies. We wonder at the seeming injustice of it; wonder how they could accommodate themselves to the loss of two, three, four of their little children.

Then there were families like that of Charles Shelly the tailor. Eight of his children reached maturity though five were dead before they reached 40. The tanner, Charles Brooker, was twice widowed, his first wife, Elizabeth, dying at the age of 30. His second wife, Ann, was only 23 when he lost her. Very frail the threads of life at this time. In 1840, 19 year old Ann Reeds, daughter of the wheelwright, died of typhoid fever, four days after giving birth to a son.

And what anguish, what horror, in this item from the Burial Register:

> "July 13, 1832 Samuel Bussey aged 21
> Buried in the night without service having died of the small pox being in a dreadful state"

The grimmest corners of our Victorian past are illuminated by marginal notes like the one above. And then there are the writers. Not Dickens alone; not just Henry Mayhew and William Booth; not just Engels and Benjamin Disraeli. None of these focuses on rural areas. The great recorders of rural life, of deprivation and decay, are Cobbett in the first quarter of the century and Richard Heath in the last. Both men are angry at what they see in terms of loss of dignity and increasing human suffering. Add to their searing prose, the graphic Reports of the Poor Law Commission in the 30s, 40s and 60s. These are the sources which give us insight into the deaths of babies and young boys and girls, which explain what it was that Joseph Cooley and Thomas, his short-lived son, and Frederick Sanger had to cope with when they ministered to their patients in Alfriston and its neighbouring parishes.

By the Victorian period, medical men had managed to shake off their somewhat louche reputations, their low-life associations with barbers and resurrection men. They had come at last to be socially acceptable, on terms sometimes with parsons and lawyers. Frederick Sanger, for example, was able to marry into the Pagden family and thus became part of the wealthy local dynasty of tenant farmers. It is a wry thought, of course, that farmers too had had to struggle for similar respectability.

Neither Sanger nor either of the Cooleys had attended medical school. The former, for example, had responded to the advertisement of Dr Skinner, a man equally untouched by prolonged medical study. Sanger had joined the elder man as an apprentice. In the 1840s, he worked from his house (Tuckvar) in West Street. From here he could look over the road to where Dr Cooley lived (Brook Furlong). Old Joseph Cooley, who had come to the parish in the previous century, had acquired his expertise in the same manner as Sanger.

By taking their place at the practitioner's side, the apprentice medico picked up his knowledge and earned his reputation by a process of observation, practice, discussion, guesswork, study, trial and error, good and bad luck. This is not to demean the work of these men; it merely puts in place the degree to which they might be competent to counter the ills they met with daily.

On their rounds, Sanger and Cooley took with them the pills they had made at home. Of course, many families prepared their own herbal cures and it is likely that some of the medicines which the doctors offered to their patients were based on country lore. Medical equipment was not sophisticated. Although the stethoscope was invented in 1819, it was not always in use in country districts. At this time, the heart was sometimes checked by the doctor putting his ear to the chest and it was for reasons of delicacy when dealing with ladies with heart conditions that he carried with him a silk handkerchief, so that embarrassment could be kept to a minimum. There was no clinical thermometer in general use until the 1860s, nor had the hypodermic syringe been invented. Laudanum alone was used to anaesthetise patients. Small wonder in a world of hack saws, when speed was impossible, that patients died of shock. The chances of the survival of many of those suffering heart attacks, thromboses, appendicitis, were often slim.

It was working conditions, the experts of the time agreed, which were often responsible for many ailments. Diarrhoea was attributed to labouring long hours in wet fields. Bad housing, as might be expected, generated all manner of diseases, according to the Poor Law Commissioners: "... fevers of every type, catarrh, rheumatism ... scrofula and pthisis which from their frequent intermarriages and their low diet, abound so largely among the poor." Many field workers suffered from chronic rheumatism, a consequence of their constant walking from an early age in heavy hobnailed boots across rough, uneven ground. Often their only protection from the elements was the sack they wore over their head and shoulders.

The only records available relating to health in nineteenth century Alfriston are in the log books maintained by the successive Masters of the village school (War Memorial Hall) from 1879 onwards, thirty or forty years after the period with which this account deals. Nevertheless, the records give some pointer to the general condition of the health of children throughout the century. They describe an endless, repetitive cycle of illness which regularly closes down the school for weeks on end or which at the very least severely reduces the numbers in attendance. It is a litany of bronchitis, scarlet fever, measles, ague, typhoid fever, chicken pox, ringworm, mumps, whooping cough, chilblains, carbuncles, boils, small pox and something referred to as "breaking out" on the face. These are not simply accounts of children's illnesses: they cannot be so airily dismissed. They are chronicles of epidemics which ate into the lives of whole families for weeks and months.

Richard Heath, that passionate observer of Victorian life, visited Alfriston and thought little enough of it. Describing the children of the poor, he wrote: "One must note the blurred eyes, the scrofulous skin, the ulcerated legs, the rheumatic agonised bodies - one must see these things and a hundred others to realise the depths of their miserable poverty." With Heath, we are of course deep into Victoria's reign but are we to suppose that things were better thirty years earlier? This is what the local doctors faced, these products of bad housing, poor food and often unhealthy working conditions. How could they ever imagine any cure for what they saw? Or if there should be a cure, perhaps they recognised that it could not come from their art alone. The pills they rolled out on their kitchen tables, the powders they mixed with well water, were frail weapons in this field.

There was work enough for the three doctors. They covered an extensive area, for none of the adjoining parishes had a medical man. There were always far-ranging calls to be made to both rich and poor, night and day. Dr Cooley senior was for many years appointed by the Vestry as Parish Doctor. For an annual fee of £10 plus additional payment for "labours, broken limbs and small pox", he attended to the poor. It is not clear how the medicine was paid for. Did the Vestry stump up? Was Dr Cooley expected to provide medicines out of his stipend? Was he encouraged, was he inclined, to withhold expensive medicines such as quinine and cod-liver oil and instead to recommend cheaper substitutes such as strong beer, wine, spirits or even mead? What could he prescribe on most occasions? Better food? Another cottage? Good working conditions? The chapel of which he was a senior member and treasurer asked for prayers one year - perhaps they asked most years - "for the Lord's Deliverance of the poor in their present depressed condition". No doubt Dr Cooley prayed fervently for his fellows not to fall ill.

Yet how odd it is. And the Cooleys and Sanger must have noticed it too. In spite of diet, housing, working conditions, the national population increased. There was a quite remarkable and unaccountable rise in births, in addition to a somewhat smaller rise in life expectancy. That Alfriston's population declined in number in the 1840s was attributable to migration from country to town rather than to fatal illnesses.

Perhaps Dr Sanger, negotiating muddy lanes on his horse as he went visiting, pondered this. And the Cooleys too.

A school was established on the Tye in 1821 in accordance with the policies of the National Society for the Promotion of the Education of the Poor in the Principles of the Church of England. It was more conveniently known as the National School and its original premises are now the War Memorial Hall. The school was not unsuccessful and continued free, part-time and voluntary until 1879 when responsibility for universal public education passed to the local School Board.

It was not the intention of those who started the school to offer more than a basic education, high on morals and deference but not disposed to disturb what was conceived to be the natural order of society. Scripture, not surprisingly in view of its link with the Church, was a significant feature of the curriculum. Huge chunks of the Bible were committed to memory quite uncritically. On the other hand, the speech of many Englishmen was moulded, as it had been for two centuries, by their acquaintance with the resonances of the Authorised Version. The speech of our semi-literate forebears was often quite unconsciously overladen with metaphor, allusion and colour from that rich source. Other elements of the curriculum included reading, writing, simple arithmetic and needlework.

It might seem a narrow enough programme but it was more than many parents had had. In the county at this time, according to the evidence of the marriage registers, no more than 30% were able to sign their names. Their signature in many cases was their sole achievement in writing. Some, of course, managed without such learning: up at William Stace's Church Farm at Berwick, the foreman, Thomas Blaber, illiterate and innumerate, kept complicated accounts in his head, though most could not shrug off such a handicap so easily.

The clergy played some part in the teaching. When the curate left the parish in 1839, he received an encomium of that glowing kind normally reserved for the newly dead.

> "We remember well," says the local correspondent of the 'Sussex Agricultural Express', "the state of the rising generation when Mr Cobb and his lady first arrived; the great good they have effected during their sojourn may be seen in the improved demeanour, intelligence, and good conduct of the cottagers' children at the present time. By personal attention and instruction they have brought about a most important and beneficial change in the children."

Added to this encouraging account is a letter purporting to be from the girls at the National School and addressed to Mrs Cobb, thanking her for her "kind and condescending manner towards them".

The Cobbs were succeeded at the school by James Richardson, a Tynesider, who lived with his wife Charity in one of the cottages facing the river. He would, within a year or two, move into the newly built house next to the school (Old School House). Florence Pagden describes Richardson as "... teacher of the ignorant on the flute, cornucopean, first fiddle, horn and bugle; brewer of small beer; Parish Clerk and half Curate; Collector of Taxes; Land Measurer; Assistant Overseer; Postmaster and Collector of Debts".

What could a man not become if he had energy and a capacity for learning?

William Wright's school in Cross House (Wood the Butcher) had been established in the village for a considerable time. Ellman, for example, claimed to have attended it. This must have been sometime in the early 1820s. The 1841 census shows three or four children staying the night at Wright's house and several other children seem to be staying in other village houses. Were these the nucleus of his pupils? Did others living at home also go to this school? Sadly, there is no evidence of numbers in attendance nor of where they came from.

There were probably one or two Dame Schools in the village. Elizabeth Smith, a widow, is described as a teacher and it may be that she taught from home. These schools had mixed fortunes. At Berwick, when Mrs Stace tried to start such a school, it failed.

Some boys probably went to Lewes Grammar School. Ellman was also a pupil there, following a very much superior kind of curriculum - Greek, Latin, ancient history, some geography even. He was later to regret very much the decline in standards at the school.

> "The cause of the dwindling of the School was principally the First Reform Bill (1832), which made a Parliamentary voter of every £10 householder, and a class of boys were admitted which lowered the whole stamp of the Grammar School. Consequently the upper classes of the Lewes residents sent their boys elsewhere."

It is a reasonable assumption that among those lowering the tone of the school were the sons of some of the superior artisans and tradesmen of Alfriston.

The dissenters in the village also established a school. Where it was held - in the chapel presumably - is not clear. What was taught, however, was probably not very different from the diet in the National School. Some of the pupils here would be the children of the craftsmen, many of whom were able to read, write and compute.

Was it an age of total belief before Darwin? When the religious census was taken of the whole country on 30th March 1851, the church authorities were alarmed at what was revealed. Only about 50% of the population attended church, a figure which, incidentally, might delight those same authorities today. Alfriston's figures are therefore particularly interesting in that they are well above the national figure.

	St Andrews	Independent Chapel
am	115 (60 at Sunday School)	150 (50 at Sunday School)
pm	185 (60 at Sunday School)	300 (80 at Sunday School)

Of course, there are questions. Were the Sunday School figures to be included in the aggregate or were they to be added on? Did some people attend both services and are they therefore counted twice? Were numbers bumped up simply because word was abroad that the census was to take place?

There being no certain answer to these questions, perhaps it is enough to say that out of a population of what was in 1851 reduced to about 600, - though doubtless there were worshippers present from other parishes just as some worshippers from Alfriston went to the churches in Lullington, Litlington or Berwick - 485 people went to chapel or church at least once on that day.

This begs the question about whether it was an age of belief. Church-going and chapel-going might have been a habit, a sign of respectability and conformity. Nevertheless, whilst accepting what lies behind that statement, many lives were touched by the teachings of the church.

The two institutions, the church on the Tye and the chapel down the twitten, underline in many ways the divisions in the country. On the one hand, the Anglican clergy was very much a preserve of the wealthy landed classes. As Heath was to write, "... the rural clergy as a class, have so closely identified themselves with the gentry as to give rise to the impression that they regard themselves as a sort of spiritual squirearchy."

Many clergy lived the life of gentry. How right Trollope is in his delineation of clerics, decent enough men for the most part, not overly concerned with affairs of the spirit, more inclined to involve themselves in the issues of their own class and their own small political universe than to be excessively committed to the whole of their flock. How else could Ellman, a good and kindly man, have come to write as he did about the effects of the Reform Bill and the consequences of allowing into the school "a class of boys which lowered the whole stamp of the Grammar School"? He was speaking about the sons of very respectable tradesmen for the most part. But did not Mrs Alexander, in her well-loved hymn of 1848, express clearly how God Himself had gone about things, the sorts of arrangements He had devised? "The rich man in his castle, The poor man at his gate, God made them, high and lowly, And order'd their estate." This was how so many saw the ordering of society.

Charles Bohun Smyth, the vicar of Alfriston, had little hesitation in describing his parish as "famous for its disaffection". He said this in 1834 when acute poverty and distress was all around him. Some years later, when he was trundled out to give church support of the Benefit Society dinner, he pronounced himself "pleased at the decorum and respectful behaviour of the members generally". If on this occasion of the dinner the farm lads drank too much, then perhaps Bohun Smyth would settle for that.

For some time Bohun Smyth did not live in Alfriston but the reason for this is obscure. But who could quibble when the majority of clergy lived elsewhere? Many, for example, were attracted to Lewes, coming out to their parishes once a week. Edward Ellman, when curate at Berwick, was never visited by his vicar, Harry West, in six and a half years. Whilst Bohun Smyth did conduct services, the various registers frequently bear the name of other clergymen taking his place. For some years he lived at the Parsonage at Litlington with his wife and three servants. Doubtless Bohun Smyth enjoyed at Litlington what he could not have in Alfriston. Here, there was no society, no great house, no squire. There were some respectable enough farmers whose writing and activities proclaim them as men of some education. They were not poor men. But they were tenants and, despite their claims, just not quite gentlemen.

At Litlington, however, the Reverend Thomas Scutt had his seat, Clapham House. Here he employed three male servants and four female in addition to farm hands. As a landowner, he was able to let out a total of 900 acres. Bohun Smyth had presumably a man of some taste and distinction as a near neighbour and as his landlord.

Ellman describes Bohun Smyth as pleasant but a trifle eccentric. He illustrates this latter quality with an appropriate anecdote. The Bohun Smyths had no children and decided therefore to adopt a child from a poor Alfriston family. The arrangements were made and the boy settled into his new home.

Presumably the Bohun Smyths were working hard at his transformation and elevation from clod to gentleman. Unfortunately, one day, when out walking with his new parents and passing his old house, the boy saw his brothers and sisters playing there. He went to join them. The Bohun Smyths, realising that in spite of their efforts they had not rid the child of his innate commonness and concluding that the condition was beyond cure, sadly returned him to his family.

What is noticeably absent is evidence of any powerful church support for the families of the poor. Where was it? Could there be such support and leadership from an absentee vicar? Thomas Geering was of the opinion that at this desperate time the church in general had no influence in the village and Heath was to charge the church with the responsibility "for the degraded condition of the English rural poor". Unlike the custom in many other European countries, and quite unlike the pastors in the dissenting chapels, the Anglican clergy did not in general spring from the homes of the poor. The Anglican clergy often did not have, could not be expected to have, considering the provenance of its members and the manner of its recruitment, any feelings for the condition in which so many of their parishioners lived.

Throughout the country, many of the poor and a significant number of artisans and shopkeepers attended chapel. In general, in Alfriston, most of the tenant farmers and their families were church-goers. John Bodle, the dairy farmer at Winton Street, had been the only Non-conformist farmer in the 1820s and 1830s. One of the James Susans, either father or son, but both shoemakers - it is unclear which and it might embrace both - was a member of Berwick Church choir. And, until his death in 1828, the wheelwright, Harry Reed, who passed on both name and trade to his son, was organist and choir master at the village church. Perhaps the other Reeds, living and working in Winton Street, were also members of the Anglican community. In general, however, families in this stratum of society tended to attend chapel.

Since 1801 the dissenters had crowded into the refurbished tallow chandlery in the twitten leading to the Tye. They had their regular helping of disagreements, disorder, schism. At the centre was that stormy petrel, Charles Brooker, who once divided the chapel over his marriage to his late wife's sister, and yet a second time, in 1839, when he and some adherents split the body. A brief reference says that a building in the main street, formerly used as a candle house, was registered for worship. Whether this means that the original chapel was re-registered or whether some other location is intended, is not clear.

In spite of the disagreements, the chapel made positive efforts to change men's lives. There are some grounds for uncertainty about the religious beliefs of the chapel members. On the one hand they claimed to believe in predestination, in the existence of an elect destined for heaven, and consequently in the uselessness of trying to alter men's ways when all had been resolved in advance. But there are inconsistencies here. Many attempts were made by chapel members to help those who had fallen from grace.

On one occasion it was resolved:

> "... that Mr. C. Brooker and Master Aucock be appointed to visit Master Foord and Wife relative to his keeping the Royal Oak Public House at Long Bridge and that they inform them that this Church consider such a situation inconsistent with the Profession of a Church Member - also that it is a source of grief to this Church to find there has not been that order in Master Foord's house which should be."

Later, the members of the Chapel expressed the hope that the Foords would do "all they can to discontinue vice and to keep good order in the house".

The records suggest that throughout the country the labouring poor tended to drink heavily. But consider their cramped homes, their dark rooms. To many, the beer house was a welcome escape, a centre of light, warmth and comfort. For their part, the dissenters disliked the excess they saw. Beer they could accept as the common drink: what they objected to was heavy drinking which ruined a man's capacity to look after his family. Their concern, regardless of any doctrine of predestination, was that a man could, should improve himself and at the least he could, by thrift, manage his affairs better. So when young John Thorncraft drank too much, other members of the chapel strove to persuade him to mend his ways. They knew him to be unreliable, knew that he worked only as and when he felt like it, that he had from time to time challenged his master's authority. Perhaps they were not surprised when he was brought to trial for the fire which destroyed three of his employer's barns at Milton Court. Of course, he had half-threatened Mr Ade on several occasions, hinted that his hay might be fired. When Thorncraft was hanged in 1831, his parents were still members of the Alfriston chapel.

But there was often joy at the thought of others recovering from their "fall and backsliding". The chapel records make several references to fallen brothers and sisters being ultimately received back into the fold.

Heath says that one day when he visited the village "the ugliest, most dismal looking building in the town, was full". It does seem that the chapel, which paid little regard to supposed advantages of birth and wealth, was successful. In its membership, it had men of some significance. Not only was there the charismatic Brooker but others including the shoemakers Haryott, Hilton, and Ridgway, Dr Cooley, Winch the cooper and Akehurst the tanner. They belonged to a dynamic and influential community as opposed to the Anglican church which in so many places was supine and inactive and which seems to have been the case in Alfriston, where even the church fabric was in a state of acute disrepair. Even to read about the church's condition suggests its symbolic weakness, although in fairness it was never an easy structure to maintain. In the 1950s and 1960s damp and beetle were still major enemies and expensive to combat. In the 1840s some of the great beams, we learn, had become old and rotten. The whitewashed walls were streaked with mould and damp. At times, water coursed down the pillars or dripped into the horse-box pews below. There were holes in the roof and so dangerous were the heavy Horsham roof slabs that many were removed to 'The George' and 'The Star'.

Compare that with the chapel whose congregation, some years earlier, had taken over the old tallow chandlery and fitted it out in a short space of time as a place fit for worship which is still used today.

It was too a matter of distance. In physical terms the vicar was distant from his church; the chapel elders were not. The vicar was distant in terms of birth, wealth and outlook; again the chapel elders were not. If there were to be any comfort in a grim world, the parish poor, by their attendance on one Sunday in 1851, suggested where that was most likely to be had.

Alfriston's leather industry which dated back to the eighteenth century flourished especially during the Napoleonic Wars. Not only were there large detachments of soldiers along the coast, in anticipation of the arrival of the French, but bodies of militia were also stationed in the village and at Winton. It was this singularly good fortune that led to contracts for gloves and leggings for the military because in the village there was an established tannery and fellmongery and a skilled leatherworking community of saddlers, harness makers, shoemakers and glovers. The decline was felt as soon as the army left. Nevertheless, for the next thirty years or so the tannery survived and the attendant skilled trades continued long after that.

The ultimate expiry of the tannery might have been due to the death in 1843 of its dynamic owner, Charles Brooker. His son, John Newman Brooker, seems to have made no attempt to revive its fortunes. Perhaps the development of other, more modern, tanneries, on a much larger scale, like those at Bermondsey, told against its future; nor is it possible to say how punishing was the boycott of the tannery by the farmers, led by Henry Pagden, who had favoured the New Poor Law and the development of Union Workhouses to which Brooker was strongly opposed. Men like Brooker arouse very strong reactions. The boycott must have damaged the profitability of the tanyard to some extent. There were other factors, too, against a rural industry which had as yet no access to a railway. Not until the late 1840s was Alfriston within easy reach of a railway line but by then it was too late. Brooker was dead, the tannery deserted, although the fellmongery which he had owned continued to operate for some years. The saddlers, glovers and shoemakers, however, still plied their trade, now seeking their materials from further afield.

In the days when the tannery was working it took all of the heavier skins, such as ox-skins, and any others requiring to be tanned. Other lighter skins - horse, calf, sheep, pig, rabbit and even those of eels caught by the Levetts of Milton Street - went to the fellmongery, which was sited by the river at the bottom of

Brooker's garden. The only man mentioned in the census as working in the fellmongery is Thomas Bussey. He is described as a fellmonger although years later, after his death, his wife calls herself "widow of a fellmonger's labourer". Obviously Bussey - incidentally, like most of those employed by Brooker, a chapel-goer - was a full-time employee. No-one else is referred to as a fellmonger. It does seem that, labourer or no, he was in day-to-day charge of the work and of any other men who came to work at the fellmongery, possibly on a temporary basis, when there was urgent yard work to be undertaken.

Whilst many skins came from the slaughterhouse, others came direct from the farms or even private homes. If an ox or sheep died on a farm or, say, a tradesman's horse died, the fellmonger or the tanner would go off to buy the skin and flaw it on site, bringing it back in the cart.

On arrival at the fellmongery, the skins were scraped clean, Bussey and whoever worked with him using two handled fleshers' knives for larger skins. Any bone or horn was set aside for John Baker, the rag-and-bone man. The bones, a source of phosphate and nitrogen, were ground down for fertiliser. At the time, the bone-grinding factory on the present Drusilla's site had not opened and it might be that Baker took his loads off to Lewes or Hailsham. As for the horn, this itself was valuable. Even the spongy interior of the horn, the flint, was sold to soap boilers. Hair and wool, of course, was used to stuff horse collars and saddlers and even cushions. Sometimes, bundles of wool were sent further afield to wool merchants, although the quantities in the Alfriston fellmongery must have been relatively small.

Somewhere in the yard, there were deep pits, brick or cement lined, in which the skins were immersed in solutions containing perhaps sulphur or lime or alum or bran. There was a variety of recipes for treating skins. After immersion, which might last for several weeks, the skins were taken out and dried by passing them through a suspended metal ring. At some stage, the skins were nailed to boards as part of the drying and stretching process. Sometimes, the skins were beaten and pulled by hand to increase their pliability.

This business of ringing and tugging and pulling clearly demanded physical strength even though the work was generally lighter than that of the tanyard. In the fellmongery, one man with a hook could lift a saturated sheepskin, although two men were required to operate the ring. Perhaps the work was spasmodic, calling for Bussey as the only permanent worker and he, when he needed assistance with the ring or the pit digging or emptying, engaged others.

After Brooker's death, the fellmongery was taken over by his executor, George Woodhams, who is described in Kelly's 1845 Directory not solely as fellmonger but also as glover, draper and grocer. Woodhams had a financial interest in gloving and fellmongery but he did not work at either of these trades. He was shortly to give them all up, emigrating to the United States. The fellmongery did not survive Woodhams' departure. As for Bussey, he is recorded in 1851 as a pauper.

As in the case of the fellmongery, many animal hides destined for the tanyard came either from Alfred Godden's slaughter house in River Lane or from the one belonging to William Banks at the back of Market Cross House. Here the skins were stripped off the carcass by strength of hand, wrist and arm. Then the fleshers' knives were used to remove the worst of any blood, veins, gristle or fat adhering to the hide. They were then trundled in a cart the short distance to the tanyard. This was located on a large site facing the river. The house in the yard (The Tanneries) was probably occupied by one of Brooker's employees. His son, John, lived at home and James Akehurst, a significant member of the chapel, is believed to have lived in the High Street. Perhaps

Samuel Sands, another chapel member, lived there with his mother, the chapel cleaner, who was also employed in the tannery.

There were two barns, one of which (The Gun Room) was separated from the main site by a walled footpath. The second barn (Farthings) was inside the main complex. Along the inside of the outer wall was a covered area where hides were hung to dry. Elsewhere, the ground was dotted with a series of immersion pits, each about six feet deep, all employed in the lengthy tanning process. Tanyards usually had channels running through them to feed the immersion pits but there is no sign of any of these today. There is a pump in the main yard and another behind the Gun Room and presumably these were used to fill the channels and pits. One wonders if skins were not taken to the river as part of the process of cleaning them.

What does remain on site is a piece of old machinery, a large rusted mystery, a complex of cogs and wheels. This was used to grind oak bark which was the essential element in tanning. Much of the bark came in huge strips from Abbot's Wood in Arlington, on Lord Gage's estate. Old Mrs Sarah Sands was responsible for cleaning it before it was put into the jaws of the machine.

The tanning process varied from place to place and from skin to skin and we can only guess at the way in which it took place in Brooker's yard. After scraping, the hides were sorted according to size and type and then the long periods of immersion in pits began.

Sometimes, the hides were soaked for two weeks in a solution of water and lime, after which they were taken out - imagine the weight of a saturated ox hide - washed and scraped again. In some tanyards the hide was placed in a pit of excrement, a rich mixture from dogs, pigs, cats, hens and pigeons. The purpose of this was to prevent putrefaction and to make the hide receptive to the bark tan. Henry Mayhew, the great observer of Victorian London, describes the pure-finders, whose calling it was to collect excrement from the streets. They sold their collections to the tanyards. Perhaps Brooker had some similar arrangement in Alfriston, whereby his pit of excrement, if he used one, was kept full.

Whatever method was used, the stench from the yard was powerfully disagreeable. When the breeze blew from the south and east, the village suffered mightily and here it ought to be added that the fellmongery was equally vile smelling. Yet against that there were said to be compensations. Tanyard workers were allegedly among the healthiest in the land. Doctors are known to have recommended that patients with lung problems should seek employment in a tanyard. When the Great Plague raged, and on the occasion of other frequent outbreaks, people are said to have taken refuge in tanyards in the belief that the fumes rendered them immune to any germs. That said, on a daily basis, the stench must have been excessively unpleasant, no matter how much more people were accustomed in those days to such rancid exhalations.

The tanning process involved immersing the skins in increasingly strong solutions of tan and water. There was therefore a regular transferring of the skins from pit to pit. Finally, perhaps after eighteen months or so, they were ready to be dried. After this, any blemishes were attended to by the currier, a member of a trade notoriously associated with deception and concealment of flaws in the hides. This was the final stage before the finished leather went to the saddler, the shoemaker or the glover.

Tanning was a business which required a heavy initial investment. Whilst Brooker's fellmongery business treated skins with more despatch than did the tannery, there is no doubt that the expenses were high. They paid off in the end of course, otherwise how could Brooker have been owner of thirteen houses in the village as well as of pieces of land? And Mrs Newman, the widow of his former partner as well as being his sister-in-law, had been able to retire comfortably, as a woman of independence, in her house (Old Apiary) in the High Street though why she should have remained so close to the reek of the tanyard is baffling. Perhaps she no longer noticed the smell. Or had she formed some sentimental attachment to the origins of part of her wealth?

Again, no evidence is available concerning the number of people employed at the tannery. Apart from the Sands, mother and son, and Akehurst, no others are named. It is only from negative evidence that we know John Brooker worked there for no other occupation appears against his name in the census. In later years, after the closure of the yard, he is described as a turner and machine maker. Any other employees, it seems, came from the anonymous ranks of labourers. Whoever they were, their employer would look for muscle for tanyard work was physically demanding, the lifting of saturated skins not a labour for the puny. Perhaps on occasion strength of arm took precedence as a qualification over regular chapel attendance. Some of the heavier skins were sent across to William Marchant's workshop (Saddler's Tea Rooms). There was a yard behind the workshop directly linked to 'The Star' backyard ('The Star' car park) and thence into Star Lane.

Marchant and his family lived across the road in a detached house (The Manor House) which at the time was divided into two, although they seem to have occupied both parts. There was a generous yard at the back of this building and it is tempting to believe that the saddler did some work there also.

In 1841 Marchant was employing two men, Thomas Ridgway and John Durrant. In later years, after her husband's death, his wife carried on the business. What is surprising is the apparently small number of people employed in such a busy trade. Marchant and his employees made saddles, harnesses for plough and draught horses, collars, leggings of hide and sheepskin, gloves for hedgers and ditchers, bags, cases, bellows for the smithy and whips. There were also repairs to be made to such items. Indeed, it is likely that repairs formed the bulk of their work.

Throughout the year, Marchant or one of his men would be called on to visit the wheelwright up at Winton Street for much of his work required leather attachments. In the spring, they would visit farms to clean and service harness. It was skilled, time-consuming work. It was not work for the casual or part-time labourers who were available in such numbers. John Durrant and presumably Thomas Ridgway, as well as their master, had served exacting seven year apprenticeships. They had learned not only to fashion or repair leather: as harness makers they worked with several materials. There were buckles, chains, bits, hooks of metal; saddles needed wooden frames; collars, like saddles, were stuffed with flock or straw or cloth.

The nagging question is how the demand for their services was satisfied. It is not as if the slack would be taken up by the opposition for there seems only to have been 70 year old Samuel Stace up at Berwick, carrying on the trade. Perhaps it was a lack of competition which enabled them to work at their own pace but that does not seem to be in accordance with the spirit of the times.

The profits from this trade were undeniably high. William Kidd had retired from the work at the age of 60 to live in West Street (Alfriston House). He rented several pieces of land and later was to describe himself as a farmer. Whether he had any links with William Marchant is not clear. It is interesting to speculate whether he had earlier run a separate saddlery from the large barn (The Forge, West Street) he owned close to his home.

Brooker, Kidd and Marchant made considerable profits from leather. At the other end of the scale were the glovers. These had always been part of a distinct cottage industry, poorer people on piece work, women often supplementing the household income. In other areas of the country, glovers made a variety of light leather goods. We hear of their making trousers, coats, breeches, jackets and waistcoats as well as gloves for balls, funerals, weddings and work. There is no specific indication of this happening in Alfriston but it would be extremely surprising if such work were not undertaken. Of course, this would imply that someone had to measure customers and do the specialist cutting necessary for garments of the kind mentioned.

Cobbett says that glove manufacture is "done in their cottages and amidst the fields ... where the husbands and boys must work". Where they do so, he says, "... the misery cannot be so great". But those involved in the trade were often poor. The association of the glovers with the poorer sections of the community is borne out by the census entries. Of the five glovers mentioned in 1841, Elizabeth Tobit, a 60 year old widow, would eventually be a pauper. The mother of Sarah Burfield, a 15 year old, was already designated 'poor'. A second 15 year old, Heiziar Levett, had parents who would soon be classified as paupers. It is likely that other women in Alfriston were employed as glovers, perhaps on a casual, part-time basis, depending upon need. Unfortunately, the weakness of the census shows up yet again, very often indicating only the employment of the male head of house.

The glovers' employer at this time was, of course, Charles Brooker although it does seem to be an error to describe his enterprise as a factory, for that implies a regularity of hours and a rigidity of organisation which is not likely to have been the case. That Brooker provided the hides, skins and pelts is undeniable: they came in the main from his fellmongery or from the tannery. That he provided some accommodation (The Perfumery) is incontestable for Florence Pagden, born in 1863, met people who recalled seeing the glovers there, stretching the leather on small stools. Of course, those working in cottage-based industries never restricted themselves to their own houses, unless heavy or cumbersome machinery was involved. Otherwise, they tended to work in each other's homes or, as Cobbett mentioned, in the fields. Perhaps it was convenient for the women to work in a room provided by Brooker. More to the point it was probably more congenial than working at home. The three females mentioned had no children to keep them in their cottages. Mary Akehurst, the wife of Brooker's young tanner, however, had three children and apparently no servant. It seems probable that she worked at home. One suspects that several other women who make no claim in the census to being glovers did so too.

The only glover mentioned in 1841 who would continue in the trade until the next census was 24 year old George Carrick who lodged with the family of an agricultural labourer. Ten years later he would be a married man with four children. Perhaps it was he who visited farmers in their homes, lawyers, clergymen, shopkeepers, any, indeed, who wished for a made-to-measure article.

The shoemakers are a most interesting group. Cobbett, with his customary assurance, says that this is "a trade which numbers more men of sense and public spirit than any other in the Kingdom". Others too make similar claims for the intellectual capacities and radical fervour of members of the trade. What we know of the Alfriston shoemakers is that several of them were self-employed; that James Sherwood employed two men; that James

Susan senior was the 1841 census enumerator and that either he or his son, James, was the local correspondent of the 'Sussex Agricultural Express'; that Richard Ridgway, described as "shoemaker of the first order", had enough property to entitle him to the vote in 1832 as had Richard Haryott; that both Thomas and Richard Hilton were house owners; that John Reed also carried on a second trade as a carrier; that when Samuel Paris died his wife took over the business. One cannot say that they were precisely as Cobbett asserted but these men and, indeed, one woman, do appear to have the independence and flair suitable to people who ran their own businesses.

Whilst made-to-measure shoes could be made for their best clients, the tenant farmers and the comfortable tradespeople of the parish who probably had individual lasts made for them, the labourers would rarely be able to hand over at once the 9s for the hobnailed boots the shoemaker kept in stock. Payment for these came usually after the harvest when the weekly wage was enhanced.

Shoemaking demanded some financial outlay for leather and returns were not always immediate. Fortunately, the shoemakers' customers were not in the main those exceptionally wealthy men and women confident enough to run up huge bills which were left unpaid for long periods. The farmers and tradesmen dealt fairly with each other; it was in their interest that they did so. And when the returns came, they were undeniably good.

It is not possible to indicate the precise economic effect of the tanyard's closure. The event does no more than highlight the transformation of the industry, its centralisation and of course its dependence upon good communications. The shoemakers in the short term survived; indeed they formed a substantial part of the national workforce. Later, they too would lose their importance as the great Midland factories superseded them. In the end, there would be a demand for local shoe repairers only; the skilled makers of shoes would yield to the machine. But as yet, tanyard or no, they continued at the trade as much in demand as ever.

METAL, WOOD AND BRICK

The blacksmith, a mythic figure, was an indispensable force within both the rural and urban economy. There were many hundreds of thousands throughout the country employed in this major trade. It was the smith's skill which kept oxen to the plough, wagons on the road, horses to the haywain. It was he who sharpened the shearing scissors or the wrought iron plough shares; who repaired the harrows, doorlatches and kettles; the horn lamps and the rails of the smart gigs in which the daughters of the wealthier farmers and the wives of professional men now flaunted themselves. One day he might be called upon to repair a gun or asked to mend a water pump in a cottage yard. Many a blacksmith doubled up as a vet, offering prescriptions and advice or even performing operations on animals.

Even in Berwick with its population of only 200, Henry White needed the help of two men at his smithy; at Litlington, with a yet smaller population, there was work enough for two smiths. Alfriston with its larger numbers had five, possibly even six blacksmiths.

One of the smithies was in Sloe Lane (Heritage Centre) where Henry Woolgar and his son Thomas worked. Another man in the trade, James Griffin, had at one time worked for Woolgar but by 1841 he was his own master. He lived at the corner of Star Lane and High Street (Steamer Trading) and his forge was in a building behind his house (Ash Barn Cottage). A document of 1871 seems to confirm this. It refers to "certain copyhold cottages one whereof is known as the 'Steamer' beer house with a large room, Blacksmith's shop and large garden thereto adjoining, situate in the High Street ... abutting on the Star Lane". In recent years, a chimney sweep visiting Ash Barn Cottage was in no doubt that the chimney there belonged to a smithy.

Both Woolgar and Griffin are listed in Kelly's Directory of 1845. So is another blacksmith, John Baker, who lived in a cottage (Quince Cottage) in Sloe Lane. Whilst there is no evidence of any forge at Quince Cottage, there must be a strong presumption of there being one on this site. Otherwise why should John Baker be listed in Kelly's which normally identifies only the self-employed? Also in the census, Charles Baker is listed as a blacksmith. Thomas Baker, living with his brother John, is not given any occupation but it can be inferred that he followed the trade of the head of the household. This appears then to be a three-man business.

The wheelwright's shop was in Winton Street. It does seem curious that its location was away from the village. There must have been some degree of inconvenience for it was at least half a mile from the nearest blacksmith. The work of smith and wright was very frequently interrelated. The reason may have something to with the billeting of soldiers at Winton Barn next to the wright's shop. Doubtless there was a constant traffic of wagons there during the Napoleonic Wars and this may account for its otherwise odd location.

The wheelwright, Henry Reed, rented his house, workshop and garden from John Bodle the cowkeeper. There is little evidence of the premises now - some remnants of a wall only - but it stood between Winton Barn and Highway Cottage. Here Reed employed both of his sons, one of them in his early twenties, the other a fifteen year old.

The wheelwright, like most of the other tradesmen, was involved in a wide variety of skilled tasks. Whilst he was asked to make carts and ploughs this was a less common element of his work because such vehicles were built to last for up to a hundred years. It was repairs and maintenance which took up the greater part of his time. Nevertheless, Henry Reed would know how to make heavy four-wheeled Sussex carts. He would certainly be asked to attend to their damaged or worn parts and to repaint them in their traditional colours of blue and red. But there was such a range of carts and wagons to attend to as the earlier reference to the Deans Place Farm inventory testifies. As there were no wheelwrights in the adjoining parishes it can be assumed that the Reeds were permanently occupied. Ploughs and harrows, new and repaired, would be dealt with in the workshop. Sometimes these would require the assistance of a blacksmith although it is quite probable that there was a tyring furnace and smithy on site as well as a lathe and drills of various kinds.

The farmers constantly needed repairs to their carts. Edward Cane would use his carts to go up to the chalk pit on the downs above his Winton Street farm. Doubtless, Charles Springate Brooker of Burnt House and the Pagdens of Deans Place and Frog Firle used theirs for similar purposes, in their case taking the chalk from the pit at the southern end of the village. There was too the constant to and fro-ing of carts to the lime pit at Alciston. All of this heavy usage on uneven ground resulted in the need for regular repairs in the wheelwright's shop.

So many people were likely to call upon the skills of the Reed family. One of the millers might ask him to fit in a new sweep to a sail or to re-cog the gear wheels of the mill; a shepherd might have prevailed upon his master to renew the mangers. Thomas Carter, the carrier in Star Lane, might need an urgent repair to a wheel for nothing must stop his daily links with the outside world. Or again, it might be a more commonplace piece of work - making a ladder for the builder, Edward Bodle.

There was of course much duplication. Not only did the wheelwright perform certain tasks which were proper to the blacksmith, others worked in wood too. Down in the village was the cooper, Ralph Winch, already in his seventies, a man who nevertheless would work for at least another ten years. His workshop was behind Alfred Godden's butchery in the High Street. Here, Winch turned out the barrels which seem so much more necessary to that age than now, an essential feature in the packing and transporting of so many items. Winch's business was profitable. He was one of those eighteen Alfriston men of substance who in 1832 was eligible to vote in parliamentary elections and he also served as a Parish Vestry member with powers to set rates to pay for the poor and for highways. Was there so much money in barrels that it conferred such powers? Probably not. But Winch was presumably more like the Hailsham cooper who, according to Thomas Geering, made pails, buckets, ox-bows, hayrakes, flour and corn shovels, box churns, ladles, dishes, spoons, trenchers and butter boards. Thus his work would overlap not only that of the wheelwright but also that of the carpenter. Indeed, in Kelly's Directory, Winch's son, George, is described as a carpenter whereas only four years earlier he is recorded in the census as a cooper. Evidently the names were interchangeable.

Several men are identified as carpenters. Among them perhaps one made furniture and if not possessed of the cabinet maker's delicate skills then at least he would be capable of turning out those sturdy oak tables and chairs referred to so often by the Poor Law Commissioners in their descriptions of the cottages of labouring families. But the work of the carpenters cannot be closely defined: it was likely to range from working with builders on the framework of houses to repairing doorposts and threshing floors which took such a heavy beating throughout every winter. Someone undoubtedly provided coffins for William Bridger who combined his High Street grocery and drapery (Tudor Cafe) with undertaking. Perhaps these items were held in stock somewhere - at Winch's? up at Henry Reed's? Perhaps not. Rich or poor, people liked a decent send-off. Where possible they liked a made-to-measure coffin of good plain elm.

As with other tradesmen, there is really no way of telling what were the carpenters' working arrangements. Perhaps some of them were self-employed: there is no available evidence of this or of the whereabouts of their workshops. Possibly some were permanently employed by the builder or the wheelwright or the cooper.

But we do know that George Ellis lived in Chapel Cottages with his wife and nine children; we know no more of John Worger than that he was the father of six; of William Levett, living in Winton

Street, we know simply that by 1851 he and his wife would be classified as paupers and that his two sons, both farm labourers, and his daughter, Heiziar, a glover, would have to help to support them or perhaps send them off to the Eastbourne Union Workhouse.

In Rope Walk, another carpenter, William Adams, lived with his daughter who is described in the census as 'independent'. Obviously, Adams had overcome his earlier difficulties. At one time, as landlord of 'The George' he had fallen foul of the law, a matter of licensing irregularities, and had served a term of imprisonment. It was Charles Brooker who had been instrumental in urging the authorities to take action against Adams, friend of Brooker's enemy, Stanton Collins.

Finally, where did the sawyer fit in? Richard Turner is the only man said to follow this trade although he must have had a co-worker to share in the brutish labours of the saw pit. There is no indication as to where he worked. Possibly he was employed by Reed the wheelwright. But there is no sign anywhere of a saw pit either up at Winton or in the village. And could anyone in Alfriston really afford to buy tree trunks to cut up and then wait for years for them to mature? More likely the wood used by the wright, the cooper and the carpenter came to the village already cut and mature. So where did Turner work? Certainly somewhere locally. His father worked on the barges and by 1851, Richard Turner was both sawyer and bargeman. More about him cannot be said.

There were several men involved in the building trade in addition to the multi-skilled innkeeper Richard Hastings, painter/plumber/glazier. But Edward Bodle alone is described as a builder. Another Edward, son or grandson perhaps, calls himself a builder improver, by which is meant that he has recently finished his apprenticeship.

Earlier in the century members of the Bodle family had been brickmakers and a deed of 1828 mentions a brickyard "lately belonging to George Bodle". The brickyard site was on the plot of ground between Dene Cottages and Fossil Cottage and stretching back and across to the present White Lodge. On the census sheet, there is a marginal note, "Brickyard", against the present Fossil Cottage. A similar note, "Brickhouse Yard" appears against the name of Dr Cooley who lived at Brook Furlong. In the apportionment register, Dene Cottages are referred to as "Brick Kiln Cottages".

In her 'History of Alfriston' Florence Pagden mentions that in the last century, during alterations to Dene Cottages, remains of a brick kiln were found. The field opposite these cottages is called Brick Kiln Brook and the high pavement from Rose Cottage to Dene Cottages is referred to locally as "down the Bricks". But brickmaking was over soon after the Napoleonic Wars.

Nevertheless there was a local demand for building. The increasing wealth of farmers was to lead to their demand for more substantial houses. Milton Court Farm is an exceptionally good example of a Victorian farm house. But the bricklayers, like others in associated tasks, were just as likely to be called out to perform less grand tasks, to point a wall or put up a brick shed. The centuries old dwellings which were rented by poor families inevitably required attention when it was no longer prudent for landlords to ignore the state of their properties.

Two families, the Wilsons and the Pettits, seem to have monopolised the building trade in the parish. The senior member of the Pettit family, 60 year old Samuel, a bricklayer, lived in West Street. With him was his son, Frederick, following the same trade. In what is now styled the Old Vicarage or in a cottage in the grounds - it is not clear which - Charlotte Pettit lived with her three sons, George, Charles and Henry, all of them bricklayers. In the cottages attached to the malthouse in the High Street (Wingrove Cottages) was yet another bricklaying Pettit, David. What cannot be discovered is whether the men in these families worked as a team.

Occupying a dwelling (The House) in the High Street was the family of the bricklayer, Richard Wilson. He was able to employ an apprentice who lived in the house with the family.

These skilled craftsmen, smiths, wrights and bricklayers, flourished at a time when other rural trades and industries suffered. The Woolgars were at their smithy well into the present century. The Reeds continued at the wheelwright's shop for many years and the Pettits and Wilson are still in evidence as local builders.

The front page of the 'Sussex Agricultural Express' for 12th October 1839 gives notice of an auction of property belonging to Mrs Sarah Brook behind whose house (Rose Cottage) was the brewery already in decline and which would soon cease functioning. The advertisement was as follows:

> "Lot 1 comprises an old-fashioned, substantial FREEHOLD HOUSE AND PREMISES, called or known by the name of the George Inn, eligibly situate in the centre of the town of Alfriston, with a frontage of upwards of 70 feet, with every convenience for carrying on an extensive business, together with a small BREWERY, both in full trade with attached Stalls, Garden and Out-offices etc., now in the occupation of Mr. John Woodhams, whose tenancy expires at Christmas 1840."

The small brewery at 'The George' was now clearly enough for the locality's needs. The one time thriving brewery behind Rose Cottage was surplus to requirements. After the sale, the tenancy of 'The George' with its brewery, presumably in the inn garden, passed to Richard Hastings, already a glazier/plumber/painter. There was nothing unusual in this multi-occupational activity. Many innkeepers carried on other trades, very frequently, though why is not obvious, as carters. Thus Hastings took on the task with typical Victorian entrepreneurial flair, with that breathtaking confidence and energy which several of his fellow villagers seemed to possess.

When, in June 1841, the Alfriston Benefit Club held its celebratory day in the village, it was attended by hundreds of people from outlying districts. Everything that day centred on 'The George'. The procession, flags waving, headed by the band, set off from the inn for the church. There appears on this occasion not to have been that drunkenness during the service which had so shocked the Reverend Edward Ellman when he preached at the celebration of 1839. But if they were sober, the members of the

Society - that doomed Society, one has to say, for twice there was too much sickness and too little subscription money and twice it was forced to close - had no need to remain so, for both 'The George' and 'The Star' were open all day as was Mr Cooley's beer shop in the High Street where beer could be bought in jugs and bottles, though not consumed on the premises. Of course, observers have remarked - they may or may not be right - that beer was the ruination of many a decent farm lad. If so, there were many ruined each Society celebration day.

In the evening of the 1841 meeting, the Society dinner was presided over by Henry Pagden of Frog Firle, Dr Sanger, his son-in-law, and the Reverend Henry Bohun Smyth. The 'Express' tells us that the company "... did ample justice to the good things liberally provided by Mr. Hastings, whose accommodation and attention gave very great satisfaction".

No doubt about it: the plumber/glazier/painter was the presiding genius. Ignore the fact that the following year the Benefit Society dinner was held across the road at 'The Star', this time with George Bodle as mine host. Obviously those who conducted the affairs of the Alfriston Benefit Society thought it diplomatic to distribute their favours evenly.

But back to the advertisement for it was not simply a public house with a small attached brewery under consideration. Lot 2 was:

> "A substantial stone and brick built FREEHOLD MALT HOUSE with tiled and slated roof, calculated to wet 10 quarters, situate at the south end of Alfriston, also in the occupation of Mr. John Woodhams, together with four Dwellings and Garden to each, attached to the above, in the occupation of good tenants, the former producing together a rental of £24. 10s. per annum."

Later in the century the four dwellings were to be transformed into part of a racing stable and then, much refurbished, both externally and internally, returned to their former use (Wingrove Cottages).

A "maultyng house" on the Tye is mentioned in a document of 1651. This description implies something of significant size, something producing malt on a small industrial scale. There were also some very small malthouses in the gardens of some houses in the village. For example, a modest domestic version stands in the garden of Clifton House in the High Street. But the term "maultyng house" suggests that malting and brewing had been on a quite substantial scale in the village for a considerable time. The advertised malthouse is undoubtedly the old "maultyng house". The stone and brick building, which for its purposes required generous floor space and room for kilns, is still attached to the cottages and is now a ladies' dress shop (Goosies).

Charles Pagden succeeded Woodhams as maltster. Like his predecessor he was a member of a prominent local farming family. The census gives no indication of who or how many were employed in the malthouse. Presumably they came from the ranks of those described as 'labourers'. They would know well the processes of converting barley into malt. They would know how to grade the barley when it came from the threshing floor and for how long it should be left in the drying kiln. These men would know the exact time the grain would need to be immersed prior to germination. This was more than a precise science: it took the confident roll between finger and thumb, the keen smell to judge flavour, the capacity to assess the readiness of the barley and its readiness to progress from one stage to another. In the humidity of the kiln, with its sour fumes, the workers went about their trade, turning the piles of germinating grain with their wooden rakes and shovels, sieving it and regulating the heat, maintaining it at about 86°, by manipulating the shutters which served in lieu of window glass.

The malt was sold to innkeepers, brewers, farmers and any others who required it. It was heavily taxed until 1860 and the local excise officer, John Dudmist, exercised supervision here. Naturally, malt was sold to 'The George' where the innkeeper brewed on the premises and there is every likelihood that 'The Star', too, brewed its own beer. Ann Foord of the 'Royal Oak' at Longbridge - the building no longer stands - was another likely customer. Where John Cooley in the High Street purchased his beer for his exclusively retail outlet is not known.

Many farmers brewed their own beer. They often produced it in three strengths, the weakest, the small beer, for women and children and for those working in their fields at harvest time. The middling strength and the most potent were doubtless kept for more worthy recipients. Cobbett frequently urged his readers to brew at home for he had little faith in the product of breweries. In his 'Cottage Economy' he offers a recipe for beer, supporting his championship of it by running down not only the dire effects of brewers' beer but also of the deplorable habit of tea drinking, especially among the poorest section of the community.

Whatever the future of the breweries, whatever the grievances of the poor, beer drinking went on unabated. Nor could all the head shaking of the chapel elders discourage even the poorest from seeking the comfort and companionship of 'The George' and 'The Star'.

MILLS AND MILLERS

Following the 1846 repeal of those laws which had until then favoured English farmers by supporting home grown corn, increasing amounts of corn began to arrive at British ports from the New World and Europe. The significance is revealed by comparing imports of grain and flour - 291,000 tons in 1843; four years later, 2,300,000 tons.

The laws had been designed in part to ensure that, in time of war, the United Kingdom would be able to satisfy its population's demand for bread. But even in peace time, so speedily had its population grown, there was in many years only a few months' reserve. Corn was dear not solely because of protective practices but because of its general shortage. And it all bore hard on the poor.

From 1846, however, with the arrival of foreign grain and developing milling facilities at quaysides, the English farmer, the miller, the mealman would date their decline. Perhaps they had assumed that the old system would last for ever, that they would preserve their monopoly and that the labourer, buying his small quantities of flour or his baker's loaf, would continue to have the worst of the arrangement.

Perhaps it was the confidence that the dependence on locally grown corn would never end that led to the erection in 1834 of the brick-built mill on Rabbit Bank, now known variously as Mill Bank, Meal Bank and Mere Bank. Daniel Sudbury, living in Waterloo Square (Post Office), operated this mill which continued working until the early years of the present century, since which time it has been converted into a house.

Also within the parish was Berwick Mill, sited a couple of hundred yards or so from Comp Barn. The miller there, William Jenner, was assisted by William Pettit and young Thomas Evernden, formerly the servant of the vicar of Berwick.

There was a wooden mill in the grounds of a house at the end of North Street. Here lived James Woodhams in the house (The Dene and Little Dene) which he rented from a relative. With Woodhams lived Henry Stace and his son Samuel. All three men were millers and Henry's wife acted as housekeeper. The mill was sited in what is now a public car park. At some stage it was removed: perhaps the one on Rabbit Bank rendered it no longer necessary. Wooden mills were frequently dismantled and moved to other sites, dragged away by huge teams of oxen. The destination of this mill and the date of its removal are not known.

At the house called Brook Furlong, which faced Woodham's mill, there was another miller, James Cooley. It is tempting to suggest that he worked at the mill so close to his home. However, it does not seem feasible: there could not have been enough work there for four men. Others have guessed that he worked at Windover Mill; certainly he did not do so in 1841, for the miller there at that time was Thomas Boys of Milton Street and he had an assistant. All that is known is that, in his later years, James Cooley had the mill at Friston.

Another of those multi-skilled men was William Banks, a relatively young man, who had already been a brewer in the village. Now he combined the trades of mealman and butcher, living next to Sudbury in one of Alfriston's biggest houses, the rabbit warren then called Market Cross House (Smugglers Inn). As mealman Banks held a powerful position: only he could sieve flour at the mill. Here was the law in action, trying to protect consumers from millers whose reputation was ever-tarnished: over the centuries there had grown with some justification serious doubts about the probity of those in the trade.

Both millers and mealmen were usually men of substance. Dealing in such vast quantities of their commodity, they needed considerable capital as well as access to banking facilities. Many of them enjoyed a relatively high status in their communities, sometimes even meriting the addition of 'Esquire' to their names and always, at the very least, 'Mister'. Often they came from financially secure backgrounds. Cooley's father was a local surgeon; the Woodhams family had farmed for centuries at Lullington Court and two members of the family were prosperous tradesmen in the village where they also owned property; up at Berwick, Jenner, from an established farming family, could afford two female servants to help his wife with their four children.

For the moment, the Corn Laws assured their comfort but when Peel reached the decision to repeal their protective barriers, his measures were to do more than split the Tory party. They were to have a resounding effect on all those whose futures and livelihood depended on corn, as well as on those who spent up to half their weekly wages on bread.

THE MISSING REVOLUTION

To what extent was the parish touched by the great affairs of the day? Certainly it felt the effects - not always happily - of better managed farming. And it sensed the distant disturbances of the period and though to a degree cut-off from the great world, it echoed the restlessness and violence of the age. In this slow world let it not be imagined that some rustic idyll was being played out. The disorders of Britain and Europe had their little imitations here.

It is remarkable, of course, that no revolution on French lines had taken place. Why had not Englishmen toppled their masters? The French had done so, had lopped off the heads of a king and his wife, of countless nobles and clergy. Even if in 1830 they were less extreme, they had sent another monarch packing. Why not here? But in France, rural Jacques was led by urban lawyers and urban artisans - there was an intellectual leadership, a political credo. Not here, where Prime Minister Wellington could take the disorders in his stride, could shrug his shoulders at the mobs, their riots, their burnings, their lawlessness in London and Nottingham, Derby and Bristol and across the rural south. "The people of England are very quiet," he had told his cabinet in 1830, "if left alone."

It is incredible. The French had not, unlike the English, lost their small farms. Over the centuries the English peasant had been reduced to being a landless labourer, wage dependent, victim of agricultural progress, victim of economic highs and lows, victim of the greed of his betters. Instead of a revolution, however, he confined himself to burning barns, maiming cattle, stealing sheep, helping himself to his master's crops. But he was only rarely violent, did not call for blood, never tried to overthrow the established order. Perhaps it is a matter of temperament; perhaps centuries of paternalism on the farm left him servile, apathetic. So in Alfriston at times there was petty crime, small vindictive disorders going back as far as 1790; in Alfriston and England there were gestures but never revolution.

In 1824, Henry Pagden at Frog Firle had complained that "for some time past he had lost divers Quantities of Oats, Barley and Peas". In later years, there were complaints in the press that Alfriston "abounded with smugglers, poachers and bad characters", warnings of shoplifters, though this must have been very small scale in an age when most items were shelved behind the counter. Lunch boxes were stolen, workers' jackets too. Copper went from the church roof. A boy, caught in flagrante, was given a months' hard labour for stealing seven apples from Charles Ade's farm at Milton Court. In 1831 a jeweller staying overnight in the village lost 481 items valued at £200.

The Whig government, associated in our minds with radical parliamentary and municipal reform, dealt with the Swing Riots of 1830 with an energy which demonstrated a concern exclusively for landowners and their tenants. These riots convulsed the south of England and the government protected its own kind. In 1831, John Thorncraft of Alfriston was hanged for arson at Milton Court. He was one of nine men and boys hanged for such offences in that year. At the same time, hundreds were imprisoned and over four hundred transported to New South Wales and Van Dieman's Land. Yet only one man had been killed in the riots and he a victim of the Yeomanry. Whig or Tory, it made no matter who governed. There were privileges to be preserved, provided they were those of the landed interest. The rural disorders were responded to with a ferocity born of panic. The rural labourer was put back in his place. With menaces.

Nevertheless, the firing, the theft, went on. The farmers were vulnerable and obliged to organise nightly patrols. At Berwick Court seven loads of wheat were set on fire and a threshing machine and several large pig pens were destroyed. In 1834, Tile Barn went up in flames and Henry Pagden lost up to £700 in damage in the course of the winter.

Despite this, for the most part the English farm labourer seems to have been exceptionally mild in the way in which he accepted his reduced state. It would be interesting to know how the rural poor really felt about those who had so treated them, interesting to know not just about their attitude to distant government but to the farmers who employed them on depressingly low wages, the root cause of their complaint. What really were their internal responses, when on occasions like the 1841 Benefit Club dinner, they heard 'the Father of the Club', Henry Pagden, refer to "the good effects produced by these valuable institutions calculated as they are to raise the character and improve the morals of the labouring classes"? Was such patronising cant accepted at its face value? Was it the bad character and low morality of the poor which had led to riots and incendiarism?

The notion of Merrie England all sounds rather hollow. It is a thing of painted masks concealing neglect as well as cruelty, ignorance in addition to viciousness and it is a thing of pain. The servility of the farm labourer which Florence Pagden describes with such approval is saddening but then she was a creature of her time. But why were our forefathers so docile, so tolerant of their despairing situation?

There is a seeming truth commented on by many writers, that the countryside was violent or at least had its own small and regular violences, as a consequence of excessive drinking. What small surplus the labourer had, we are told, went on drink. The small local struggles in the 1820s between Charles Brooker and Stanton Collins had to some extent, drink as one of the causes of their disagreements. Collins, the butcher, is known chiefly for his smuggling activities although it may be that legend overpowers reality. But Collins was at the centre of a lawless coterie who met at 'The George' and who laid plans there for further thefts. Brooker's stiff-necked chapel views could not easily be accommodated in so small a village alongside those of Collins. First of all there was a court case, brought by Brooker, in which a girl employed by the parish was said to have been raped by Collins. The case came to nothing.

Brooker turned his attention to William Adams, licensee of 'The George'. When charges relating to his licence as a publican were brought by Brooker, Adams was sent to prison. An explosion at Brooker's tannery might have been a response at Collins' instigation. This struggle, between what might have been regarded as between Right and Wrong or Freedom and Liberty or Narrow Chapel against Free Floating Anglican, ended with Collins' transportation for the theft of barley from a barn on the Tye.

Stanton Collins does in fact seem to have represented and encouraged criminality. His smuggling might have been quite acceptable: were smugglers not described as "honest thieves"? His theft of sheep and crops were more directly against his fellow parishioners. This could never be regarded as acceptable. In this narrow community, who could have felt safe against a relatively wealthy, intelligent young man, determined to enrich himself at the expense of his neighbours? Nevertheless, Collins' departure from the scene did not end such lawlessness. John and James Huggett were transported for sheep stealing in 1835. Three other men received similar sentences the next year for similar offences. And so it went on.

There continued down the years a succession of attacks on property. But it was not a revolution; no wealthy man lost his head or his land. They were reminders only that the rural worker had lost his birthright in earlier times and that now he lived a life that was sometimes cruel, often sad and usually harsh. As one of them was later to say: "It wasn't a livin'. Only a bein'.".

Yet if disorder was not always in the forefront, it was never completely absent from the background. But really it was more a snarl than a full-throated cry of rage.

THE LABOURING POOR

There is a tendency to think of the rural labouring poor as those working on farms. Inevitably so, because the great reports of the Poor Law Commission tend to focus exclusively upon agricultural labourers, then the largest industrial group, and we therefore know more about them than any other section of the community. But there are others to take into consideration. There were the men who worked on roads and those who did unskilled tasks in the tannery, the malthouse, the fellmongery; there were those who rarely worked, relying on parish hand-outs; there were the permanently sick, the terminally ill, the frail, the crippled and those who had, after a lifetime of labour, little strength left for work. The labouring poor was a great number of people, well over fifty per cent of the population for it included wives and large families.

Why then leave this huge class to the end? Perhaps because it seems to carry the whole burden of blame; perhaps because it seems to carry all the responsibility for its own worthlessness. It is this class which is allegedly idle; which lives off the parish; which eats the wrong food; which mismanages its money; which is dirty; which cannot cook food properly; which is responsible for any lawlessness. So we are told.

The real crime of the labouring poor was that it was too populous. There were just too many people and too few jobs. And Commissions will tend to apportion blame when they come ultimately to investigate such circumstances. Sadly, the blame will be directed at those least able to remedy matters.

The information in the 1841 census suggests that some men were permanently engaged in farm work. With the exception of the shepherds, however, it is not possible to know precisely the work these men did. Somewhere under the blanket title of "agricultural labourer" were men who knew about horses and oxen, who had mastered the plough, who laid hedges, drove carts, managed cattle, repaired barns, worked with harrows, scythes and carts. There were such men, with a sensitive, well-honed awareness of their craft.

Fifty adult men and thirteen boys are designated as agricultural workers. But the census is an often uncertain source of information and there is the possibility of several more men and as many as sixteen boys working regularly on farms. It is especially galling that in 1840 the parish did not complete and return a questionnaire from the Poor Law Commission which would have given rather more precise data, including information about wages and hours. Unfortunately there was a great resistance on the part of parishes to governmental interference. The Overseers in Berwick and Glynde, however, submitted replies and the necessarily rough assessments for Alfriston are based on their estimates.

Among the seemingly permanently employed was William Haryott who had a cottage on Frog Firle farm. It is therefore a safe assumption that he worked for Henry Pagden to whom he paid rent, perhaps 1s a week, for his accommodation. With Haryott lived his son, Harry, another worker on the farm. In another of the cottages, John Levett the shepherd, lived with his two sons, both of them also farm hands.

Down the road at Burnt House were other labourers, housed in cottages. These included James Aucock, Robert Reeds and Charles Marchant whose two sons, aged 12 and 14, worked with their father. At Winton, several families of workers were accommodated in farm cottages. In one of them was the shepherd, Thomas Tucknott.

Whilst it is possible to identify a few of the farm workers and their homes, in most cases it cannot be done. The location of the homes of other working men too are equally uncertain. Most of them lived in the village, tucked away in the dark cottages of the High Street and Waterloo Square. What does seem sure is that the minority of those identified as living in farm cottages were likely to be the only ones in permanent work. The shepherds were certain of a place and so perhaps were others such as horse men, hedgers and others deemed specialists, men whose tasks were regarded as central to the success of the farm. No other employers provided accommodation for their workers. There was nothing for brewery hands or tanyard workers: they and most others had to seek homes to rent on the open market, owned for the most part by farmers and tradesmen.

It would seem that on Alfriston's four principal farms - in all, about 2,155 acres - there was work for some of the year for up to about seventy men and boys. But so much depended upon the particular season of the year; the weather, the acreage given to pasture as opposed to arable: the price of corn; and, of course, the capacity of some farmers to so regulate their activity that there was always some work available. The root of the difficulty was that a growing population, along with more efficient farming, led to a glut of labour at many times of the year. Only at harvest time was the slack taken up for then every available man, woman and child was called upon to help and even workers from outside were often employed. But at other times weather could limit work and therefore wages; winter could lead to lay-offs; bad harvests - and there were several in these years - had their damaging effect.

Much farm work was now contracted out. A man and a boy, for example, might be engaged to dig an acre of land for a fixed sum of money. Before harvest, boys were employed to scare birds at a rate of 4d or 6d for a twelve or fourteen hour day. Some eight year olds weeded for twelve hours, at the end of the day being paid 3d; children of this age operated turnip cutting machines and there was always a call for boys to mind horses or to goad ox teams during ploughing. In the winter, if their fathers were fortunate enough to find three or four months' work - back-breaking work - flailing on the threshing floor, boys would make the work easier and quicker by laying out the sheaves in the right place.

Women were seasonal workers. With their children, they weeded in spring; helped with the hay; reaped and gathered corn at harvest time; picked stones; and in winter, they collected and spread cattle droppings from the yard into the fields. But mainly, whenever they worked, the women were constantly stooping, bending, their bodies constantly aching. It was unremittingly harsh labour.

There were complaints about the idle young, their predisposition to crime. But young single men experienced difficulties in finding work. The farmers found it to their advantage to employ married men with three children. Such men could be employed for part of the week on a low wage and the deficit made up from the Poor Rate. Not unnaturally the shopkeepers and tradesmen who contributed to the Poor Rate were incensed when this occurred. They could not accept the justice of subsidising the farmers' labour costs.

The best many a family could expect to live on was about 12s a week, yet real wages of the labouring poor, according to reliable estimates, fell usually between 7s and 10s. According to Thomas Geering who was born in Alfriston and who, although he lived most of his life in Hailsham, never lost contact with the village, was of the opinion that the Poor Rate was much abused but he did not hold the farmers responsible for this. In his view, it was the fault of the indigent poor.

> "Men in the full vigour of life did not hesitate to throw themselves on the parish. Relief in money or kind, or both, could not be refused. Self-help was not understood among our labouring population, neither was the glorious privilege of being independent recognised: we were in an abyss of degradation and moral degeneracy."

If this were even partly true, perhaps it could be understood. But the fact was that no matter how he might seek by his own efforts to elevate himself, the rural labourer, the Alfriston lad, working in the fields or on the roads or in the tanyard, would rarely receive enough in wages to do more than support himself and his family in a subsistence economy. Under this system a man could not fall too far: he would be borne up by parish relief. Yet he could not rise too high, his meagre wages ensured that. Thus, the incentive to work, the ability to make himself independent and to relish the privilege was denied him. What was created was a benefit dependent society which stifled hope, ambition and the possibilities of improvement.

No figures for wages paid in Alfriston parish for full-time work are available. At Glynde, however, 12s per week was said to be the usual summer wage with a harvest bonus of 1s 6d per week plus beer. In winter when there was less opportunity for work, the wage was lower.

At times, of course, the labourer and his family were sought after. Nothing shows up the imbalance in the labour supply as much as the contrast between winter and haymaking and harvest times. In summer, all over the country, small communities like Alfriston, using working methods similar to those described in the Bible, set out to satisfy the needs of a growing industrial nation. In one part of the country there are complex, steam driven machines being manufactured; there are clattering shuttles and endless motion of machine driven looms. Railway mania grips the land; Brunel's steamships crossing the Atlantic hint at the future. Britain is on the verge of becoming the Workshop of the World. In another part of the country, men, women, children, armed with rakes or swap hooks, scythes and sickles, collect hay for winter feed or gather in the corn. Nor is there any instrument or tool in these fields that could not have been seen a thousand years before.

Now teams of men, four or five of them, will contract to scythe a field. They will work from early light until dusk, and their wives and children will rake and help load the wagons. With luck enough winter feed for cattle will be assured. There is never too much here in corn country. For much of the year the cattle are pastured in the water meadows, in Little Brook and Egle's Brook, Large Cow Brook and The Ham, The Tye and Crosway Brook, but in winter these flood. The haymaking needs to ensure that all will be well.

In the four or five weeks of harvesting all hands will again be needed, working every possible hour. There are never enough people for the tasks which need to be done. Never enough hours.

> "The man and the boy go to work generally about 4 o'clock," a witness reported to the Poor Law Commissioners in 1843. "The common rule is you should not leave off reaping till you can see a star."

But the really common rule was reap while you could and that was determined by the weather. Even so, labour had often to be imported in order to complete the work as quickly as possible. Later in the year there would be insufficient work, insufficient food for the village's families.

After the harvest, a bonus was paid. As a result there was often enough to pay off arrears in rent, arrears for groceries; enough to pay for a new pair of boots or gaiters or corduroy trousers. But when it came, the bonus did not stop the year-long wretchedness: it merely prevented its worsening.

Then there was the leasing or gleaning at the end of the harvest. When the farmers agreed, the families were allowed into the fields to collect what remained of the ears of corn. What they carried off was threshed at home and in Alfriston was ground into flour not at the mill but in the house where many families had their own hand querns. As for the chaff, this was used to stuff mattresses.

The savings from the leasing were not inconsiderable. A family might grind enough flour to last them several weeks, a significant saving when bread cost perhaps as much as fifty per cent of a poor man's wage. But any savings would flow out again, along with the money made at harvest. It was all spoken for, this money; it always would be for these families.

Much expenditure went to travelling packmen who visited the village with remnants and scarves and lengths of corduroy, offering packets of pins and thread and ribbons. At other times, some families stocked up from the stalls at the annual fair. Yet others paid the tally man for their cheap and shoddy goods. There was a tendency not to buy in the local shops if at all possible for these, with little competition, asked notoriously high prices. Yet where else could a local family buy their few groceries if not locally? Would a shop in some distant village offer credit? There was only a feeble shop at Berwick to go to with few enough goods to sell. Who would walk that far to pay just as much?

Of course, the criticism of how the poor conducted themselves went on unabated. If they lived badly, it was their own fault; they laid out their money foolishly; they ate the wrong kinds of food; they could not cook. The Poor Law Commission said that of them and in the early years of this century, Arthur Beckett, visiting Alfriston, complained:

> "The women have yet to learn the art of cooking vegetables - their boiled cabbage is detestable and the smell of it scents the cottage long after it has been consumed."

It was of course easier for a wealthy newspaper owner to comment on how poor people lived.

The following example, taken from the 1843 Poor Law Commission report, gives an indication of how one family budgeted for a week on 12s:

6 gallons of flour	8s 0d
½ lb soap	0s 3½d
3/4 lb candles	0s 4½d
1 lb butter	1s 0d
¼ lb sugar	0s 2½d
1½ lb meat	0s 9d
yeast	0s 3d
starch, pepper, salt	0s 2d
1 lb cheese	0s 6d
worsted, cotton, tape	0s 3d
	11s 9½d

So, in this corn growing area, over fifty per cent of earnings goes on flour. Is it good quality or is it 'sharps', the cheap adulterated variety? And milk? Perhaps there is a prejudice against it as there was in many rural areas. Is the baby given 'pap', bread soaked in hot water, in preference to milk? And though they love their tea, does this family do the same as some others? Do they add boiling water to burnt toast and persuade themselves that it is as good as tea? And what about kindling? Clothing? Workboots at 9s a pair? And work gaiters? And rent at 1s or 1s 6d a week? When will all this be paid off? After haymaking and harvest? Will the landlord, the grocer, the shoemaker, the tailor, the tally man swallow up the summer bonuses all in one gulp? Assuming they do, will there ever be any saving? Will it always be debt? And what will happen in old age?

The supreme humiliation for many was entry to the workhouse, that reform conceived in the hard inhuman spirit of modern science, according to Richard Heath. Small wonder that several men well into their seventies continued working while they could. Thomas Worger (80) and Joseph Bedwell (70), for example, were employed on farms. Yet, the tenders for Eastbourne Workhouse ask for "flour, boneless beef, neck of mutton, suet, cheese, butter, good black tea, sugar, oatmeal, soap, candles, salt, pepper and furze faggots". Would this not have tempted some? Here was feeding and warmth beyond dreams. Yet the poor resisted it. It was not solely the grudging nature of the system which fuelled this resistance, but its indiscriminate collections of humanity, the luckless along with the feckless, the hard-done-by along with the ne'er-do-well, the good and the vicious, side by side. Yet, not side by side with their wives, their own children. The ultimate cruelty was segregation, the wrenching apart of families. It was not the intention of the new Union Workhouses to be kind, warm, welcoming. Their policy was to deter what was construed as idleness.

In Alfriston, there was a powerful voice against the system of relief as it was now applied. Charles Brooker, combative, opinionated, difficult, called out against a regime which inhumanely separated man from wife, child from parents. Brooker had attempted to gain election to the Board of Guardians of the Eastbourne Union in order to work from within, either to improve or destroy the system. Local farmers led by Henry Pagden favoured the arrangements, however, believing that it would reduce the burden of the Poor Rate. They succeeded on a technicality in denying Brooker his place on the Board. It may be, however, that Brooker's advocacy - and he was a powerful speaker and preacher - persuaded local people to continue to look after their dependants with some assistance from the parish. In 1842, a powerful leaflet written by Brooker and addressed to 'Tradesmen and Working Men, particularly Agricultural Labourers' attacked further Poor Law legislation. The tanner's strongly held beliefs come over all too clearly.

> "The Landowners, Clergy - and too much Dissenting Ministers - and Farmers generally, have by their procedure gone to uphold the New Poor Law: and the Farmers above all others have disgraced themselves by the dreadfully harsh manner in which they have upheld, in which they have worked the New Poor Law. Have not these Farmers now through their Guardian-Board-working of this inhuman, heaven-defying, and murderous New Poor Law, got you so under their power that you are almost afraid of looking

them in the face for fear of being sent, if you offend them in the least, to a Poor Law Bastille, to a murder-den-Poor Law Union Workhouse."

Powerful indeed and deeply felt.

The people Brooker had in mind were those like 80 year old George Tucknott, described as "poor", who stayed with his son, Thomas, the shepherd, up at Winton Street. Another was Lucy Martin, a poor widow aged 30, who lived with her son Absolom (15), a farm hand; it was his wage - perhaps 6s per week - and her relief which kept them and three young children from starvation.

Richard Wilson, the bricklayer in the High Street, looked after not only his parents and family but also an aged pauper, Benjamin Bussey, whose wife, Sarah, lived with another bricklayer, David Pettit, in his High Street house (Wingrove Cottages). Perhaps both Pettits and Wilsons were related to the Busseys. The complex marriage patterns, the series of intermarriages in the village, obscure any precise relationship. The Pettits, Wilsons and Busseys were certainly all members of the chapel and, as such, disinclined to marry outside of the membership, so that there is likely to be a relationship. Or, perhaps they were simply putting into practice that charity towards the aged which Brooker and his chapel believed ought to emerge directly from the community, rather than from the anonymous, cold handed workhouse.

Elizabeth Smith, a 70 year old schoolmistress - though where and whom she taught is not known - had two middle-aged daughters to maintain. Both are described as "poor". Why were those women unable to fend for themselves? Had they been brought up in too genteel a fashion? Did they both suffer from some unspecified handicaps? What is interesting is that they were still at home in the care of their mother and that they, rather than their mother, should be so identified.

Heiziar Levett, the 15 year old glover, was in 1841 helping to support her mother and younger sister. Nearby, 85 year old Richard Reeds lived with his son-in-law, a labourer. In a cottage behind the High Street (behind 'Sally's'), 80 year old William Vinall lived with his wife (75) and Mary Swadling (65). Each was described as "poor", legitimate recipients of what the Poor Rate could afford to offer them. 80 year old Sarah Pettit is the only poor person living alone. It may be safe to believe that at least one of the large Pettit family looked after her.

In the early Victorian period, life worsened for many men, women and children in Alfriston. Until relatively recently the parish had been cushioned from the worst economic hazards that had already visited other parts of England and indeed the county. The decline of its brewery and its tannery and all of the attendant benefits springing from these were, by the end of the third decade, to lead inexorably to a worsening of conditions. By 1851, even more men and women would be declared paupers. In the preceding century, life for the labouring poor had been hard but bearable; now it was looked back upon with a kind of wistful regret. In those days, often under paternalistic regimes which treated the rural labourers as children, they had a roof over their heads, food in their bowls and clothes on their backs. Now, there was no guarantee of any of these.

Both Geering and Heath reflected on what, by the last quarter of the century, Alfriston had become.

> "Nothing remains to occupy its inhabitants," Heath wrote, "but agricultural labour ... Ignorance dense and dark seems to have settled on the place."

And Geering regretted what had become of his birthplace:

> "Ultimately the brewery rotted to the ground, and the vaults and cellars became a retreat for dogs and truant boys to skulk in. The brewers' occupation was gone, there being not enough mouths to drink nor money to pay for the beer and so what befell the brewhouse followed and swept away all the other principal trade buildings. The fine tannery became a desolation and the workmen drifted away into other occupations and other homes; and so it has come about that the grocer, the shoemaker and one or two minor callings are all that is left of the once flourishing trade of Alfriston."

The almost self-sufficient village had finally disappeared.

REFLECTION

When I come to consider it, I liken this account to a kind of jigsaw, of which the outer edges are neither regular nor parallel; of which the pieces are ill-fitting or missing; of which the colours, instead of being of a luminous richness, are often simply muted shades of grey.

I find I have neglected all mention of geese in lanes and hens in gardens; there is nothing about horses staring over village walls or sheep enclosed in the plots and orchards of our small township. There is no echoing laughter from inns or cottages or fields. But it cannot have been complete gloom; there must have been tenderness and graciousness here, cheerfulness and contentment, though I have recorded none. Because, of course, these were bad years, when an English village lost its self-sufficiency and there was no longer any guaranteed place for the countryman in fields that had once belonged in part to his forefathers.

I hope, in spite of the above, that I have produced some kind of representation of the past in this parish. The best I can hope for is that it is a roughly correct picture. It is full of conjecture; "likely" and "perhaps" stud my text. There are great gaps in my knowledge, partly because of the absence of documentation relating directly to Alfriston. The consequence has been that I have had to rely on references to other places during the period. Even our local industries, the declining tanyard and brewery, have had nothing written about them and I have had to turn to what has been said of similar industries elsewhere.

So then, I offer this tentative fragment of our parish history in the hope that it will shed some faint light on our past and may serve to stimulate others to add more definition to what I have produced.

BIBLIOGRAPHY

Manuscript Sources

Census	1841
Tithe Map and Apportionment Register	1843
Baptismal, Marriage, Burial Registers	1813-1854
Minutes of Independent Chapel	1801-1837
Vestry Minutes	1623-1825;1849-1879
School Log Book	1879-1908

Newspapers

Sussex Agricultural Express	1837-1854
The Times	1830-1854

Reports of the Poor Law Commission

The Administration and Practical Operation of the Poor Law, 1834
The Sanitary Condition of the Labouring Poor, 1837-1847
The Employment of Women and Children in Agriculture, 1843

Books

Arthur Beckett, The Spirit of the Downs, Methuen, 1909
Nathaniel Blaker, Sussex in Bygone Days, Combridges, 1919
Donald F Burgess, No Continuing City, Privately printed, 1985
William Cobbett, Rural Rides, Vols 1 and 2, Culley, 1909
John C Egerton, Sussex Folk and Sussex Ways, Chatto & Windus, 1892
Edward B Ellman, Recollections of a Sussex Parson, Skeffington, 1912
Thomas Geering, Our Sussex Parish, Methuen, 1925
Richard Heath, The Victorian Peasant, Sutton, 1989
Hobsbawn and Rudé, Captain Swing, Penguin, 1973
Thomas W Horsfield, A History of Sussex, 1835
Richard Lower, Stray Leaves from an Old Tree, 1862
John Lowerson, Victorian Sussex, BBC, 1972
E & M McCarthy, The Cuckmere: Another Sussex River, Lindel, 1981
Florence Pagden, History of Alfriston, Combridges, 1895
A Cecil Piper, Alfriston, Muller, 1970
Maud Robinson, A Southdown Farm in the Sixties, Dent, 1938
Denys Thompson, Change and Tradition in Rural England, CUP, 1980
G M Trevelyan, English Social History, Longmans, 1944
J A Vickers, The Religious Census of Sussex 1851, SRS, 1989
Roger Wells, Popular Protest and Social Crime (Southern History Vol 13), 1991
Barclay Wills, The Downland Shepherds, Sutton, 1989
Arthur Young, A General View of the Agriculture of Sussex, Sherwood, 1813

Other Sources

Kelly's Directory, 1845
Sussex County Magazine, Vols 1-30, 1927-1956
Ordnance Survey Map, 1874